more veg less meat

More veg less meat

The eco-friendly way to eat, with 150 inspiring flexitarian recipes

Rachel de Thample

Photography by Peter Cassidy Illustrations by Tim Hopgood

Kyle Books

For my lovely husband, Robbie,
and my little cook, Rory.

This paperback edition published in
Great Britain in 2018 by Kyle Cathie Limited
Part of Octopus Publishing Group Limited
Carmelite House, 50 Victoria Embankment
London EC4Y 0SZ
www.kylebooks.co.uk

First published in 2011

10 9 8 7 6 5 4 3 2 1

ISBN 978-0-85783-464-5

PROJECT EDITOR: Jenny Wheatley
COPY EDITOR: Liz Murray
PHOTOGRAPHER: Peter Cassidy
ILLUSTRATOR: Tim Hopgood
DESIGNER: Lawrence Morton
FOOD STYLIST: Linda Tubby
PROPS STYLIST: Roisin Nield
EDITORIAL ASSISTANT: Estella Hung
PRODUCTION: Gemma John

A Cataloguing In Publication
record for this title is available
from the British Library.

Printed and bound by Toppan
Leefung Printing Ltd in China.

Contents

INTRODUCTION

One of the first things many people said to me when I told them about this book is: 'Well, I don't really eat that much meat.'

That is exactly what I thought when I first started seeing 'Eat Less Meat' in newspaper headlines, but I was surprised when I calculated just how much meat my family consumed. What really startled me was when I factored eggs and dairy into the equation. They, too, have major implications for our health, the environment and animal welfare.

Just think: the milk in your latte, the slice of cake you have with it (probably made with eggs and butter), your breakfast yogurt. It starts to add up. Never mind the full cooked breakfast.

In the United Kingdom, where I live, Britons consume twice as much protein as they need. Much of it comes in the form of meat and dairy. In 2002, the average Briton ate 80kg of meat and 10.2kg of cheese – equivalent to 1,400 pork sausages and 40 blocks of Cheddar.

In America, where I'm from, meat consumption is even higher. The average American eats an average of 125kg of meat each year – equivalent to more than 400 sirloin steaks.

In the second half of the 20th century, worldwide meat production increased roughly five-fold; per capita consumption more than doubled.

To keep up with such meat and dairy-heavy diets, animals are intensively reared. The bulk of these animals do not live on what we would call farms. Quite often these animals don't see the light of day, and they are not fed the diet that nature intended for them. Eating food from such animals cannot be good for our health. Rising obesity levels, increasing cases of cancer, heart disease and diabetes show that it's not.

This book is all about making small changes that will have a huge impact on your health, the wellbeing of the animals, and the environment.

You don't have to transform the way you eat. The recipes in this book avoid gimmicks: no fake bacon or soy cheese. They're familiar everyday favourites like burgers, pizza and pasta. They just have a bit less meat and more veg.

Following the best nutritional guidelines, I've created a formula for the recipes. Each one has no more than 50g of meat, dairy or eggs per serving, and most offer half your recommended five portions of fruit and veg a day.

Buying a chicken and making it last a week or trimming a steak to make a meal for four will also save you money. One of the best things you could do is to reinvest your savings in better quality meat. Each chapter outlines the health benefits of trading up, and includes great sourcing tips.

Why 50g?

Nutritional guidelines say we only need an average of 50g of protein each day – a little bit more for men (56g), slightly less for women (45g). This small amount is all we need to stay healthy and energetic. One chicken breast offers the full amount, so this alone will make you protein fit for the day. However, you don't even need this much meat to satisfy your needs as just about every food has a bit of protein in it, even strawberries.

Protein deficiency is extremely rare in the Western world. In fact, it's more common for people to suffer from eating too much protein. Excessive intake can lead to high blood pressure and kidney problems, making health a compelling motive to eat modest amounts of protein-rich foods such as meat and dairy.

The world's leading medical journal, *The Lancet,* did an in-depth study on the amount of protein we get from meat. It looked at both the health and environmental impacts of

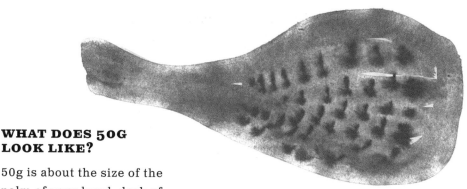

WHAT DOES 50G LOOK LIKE?

50g is about the size of the palm of your hand, deck of cards or...

1 chicken drumstick or thigh

½ small chicken breast

About ⅓ fillet steak

1 lamb chop or cutlet

1 medium egg

4 heaped tablespoons of cheese

our meat consumption and concluded that we should limit our daily intake to 90g. The authors of this report are currently looking at suggested limits on dairy and eggs as well. Other reports already have. One extensive paper, 'Cooking up a storm', produced by the Food Climate Research Network Centre for Environmental Strategy at the University of Surrey, ultimately concluded that we should look at reducing the amount of food we eat from *all* animal sources, including fish, dairy and eggs.

To sum up, our diets are heavily reliant on animals, something that we clearly need to reassess. Taking the aforementioned research into consideration, I've designed each recipe to contain no more than 50g from an animal source, the idea being to eat two meals containing this portion per day as well as one plant-based meal.

Readjusting the balance on our plates doesn't mean you should feel deprived. There are some seriously meaty dishes in this book, such as the Beef Carpaccio on page 37, the Shepherd's Pie made with roast lamb and dripping on page 54 and the BLT on page 79.

Trimming the meat in all of these recipes has made space for more fruit and vegetables, which are another key feature of this book. We eat too much meat and too little veg. Striking the right balance is good for you, the environment, and the animals which provide us with food.

Why 5 A Day?

The World Health Organisation (WHO) recommends that we consume at least 400g of vegetables per day. One portion of veg equals roughly 80g, giving us a 5 A Day goal to work towards. However, a recent report by the World Cancer Research Fund and American Institute of Cancer Research recommends an even higher intake of fruit and vegetables: 600g of fruit and non-starchy (i.e. green leafy) vegetables and at least 25g of other plant-based foods (such as nuts, seeds and legumes) daily to protect against cancer.

The bottom line here is that we need to eat as much fruit and veg as we possibly can. Whether or not we need to eat meat can be debated between carnivores and vegetarians until the cows come home but the fact that we need to eat lots of fruit and vegetables is undisputed.

According to the UK's Department of Health:

'Increasing fruit and vegetable consumption is considered the second most effective strategy to reduce the risk of cancer, after reducing smoking. In particular, people who do not eat fruit and vegetables regularly are at greater risk of several common cancers, including colorectal and stomach cancers. There is evidence that people who eat at least five portions of fruit or vegetables a day are much better protected against cancer and heart disease than those who don't.'

Many of us across the Western world are not even making a dent in the WHO's original 5 A Day goal, so I think it's a good minimum to work toward. When we get there, we can start bumping our intake up more and more.

Following the recipes in this book will help you make great strides towards the WHO's recommended 5 A Day. Most of them will get you halfway there. As well as vegetable-rich main dishes, I've included fruit-laden desserts and breakfast options to help you increase your intake even more. It's a delicious, colourful way to eat and you'll feel all the better for it.

WHAT EQUALS 1 OF YOUR 5 A DAY?

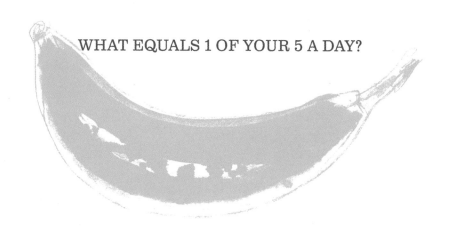

Apple	1 medium apple		Courgettes	½ courgette
Apricot	2 fresh or dried apricots		Chard	2 leaves of chard
Artichoke	1 freshly cooked globe artichoke or 2 marinated artichoke hearts		Chickpeas	5 tablespoons
			Chicory	½ head of chicory
Asparagus	5 chunky spears / 8–10 thin spears		Chinese leaf	3 leaves
			Clementine	2 clementines
Aubergines	⅓ aubergine		Cranberries	1 large handful or about 20 berries
Avocado	1 small or ½ large avocado			
Bananas	1 small banana		Cucumber	⅓ large or ½ smaller cucumber
Beetroot	½ large or 1 small beetroot			
Blackberries	7 larger / 9 smaller berries		Dates	2 dates
Blueberries	½ cup or about 30 berries		Fennel	⅓ fennel
Broad beans	5 tablespoons, or the beans from 7–8 pods		Figs	1 plump fresh fig or 2 dried
			French beans	A fist full of beans or 14 beans
Broccoli	5 chunky florets			
Brussels sprouts	5 sprouts		Gooseberries	½ cup or 15 gooseberries
Butternut squash	¼ medium squash		Grapes	15 grapes
Cabbage	⅛ head of cabbage		Grapefruit	½ large grapefruit
Carrots	1 medium carrot or 2 small carrots		Jerusalem artichokes	4 larger Jerusalem artichokes
Cauliflower	5 florets		Kale	3 tablespoons finely chopped kale or 2 whole leaves
Celeriac	⅛ celeriac			
Celery	2 sticks celery		Kiwi fruit	2 kiwis
Cherries	10 cherries		Kohlrabi	½ kohlrabi

Leeks	½ leek
Lemon	150ml juice
Lettuce	4–5 large leaves of lettuce or 1 cup smaller leaves
Lentils	5 tablespoons cooked lentils or a handful dried lentils
Mango	⅓ mango
Marrow	⅛ marrow
Melon	⅓ melon
Mushroom	1 portobello mushroom, 6 chestnut mushrooms, or 1 large handful wild mushrooms
Nectarine	1 large or 2 smaller nectarines
Onions	1 medium onion
Orange	1 orange
Pak choi	3 larger or 4 smaller pak choi leaves
Parsnip	1 smaller or ½ large parsnip
Peas	5 tablespoons frozen or fresh peas
Peaches	1 peach
Pears	1 small pear
Peppers	½ pepper
Pineapple	⅙ large pineapple or ¼ mini pineapple
Plums	2 plums
Pomegranate	½ pomegranate
Porcini	2 large fresh porcini (ceps) or a small handful dried
Prunes	2 prunes
Pumpkin	⅙ large, ¼ medium or 1 mini pumpkin
Quince	½ quince
Radicchio	3 leaves of radicchio
Radish	5 radishes
Raisins	1 heaped tablespoon raisins
Raspberries	5 tablespoons, or about 20 berries
Red cabbage	⅛ head of cabbage
Red currants	5 tablespoons currants
Rhubarb	2 sticks rhubarb
Rocket	2 large handfuls rocket
Runner beans	3 runner beans
Salsify	2 sticks salsify
Samphire or other fresh seaweed	1 handful or ½ cup
Shallots	4 small shallots or 1 banana shallot
Spinach	3 large handfuls raw spinach or ½ cup cooked spinach
Spring greens	3 larger spring green leaves or ½ cup chopped spring greens
Spring onions	6 spring onions
Squash	½ smaller summer squash or ⅙ medium-sized pumpkin like autumn squash
Strawberries	5 berries
Sugar snap peas	15 peas
Swede	⅙ larger or ¼ smaller swede
Sweetcorn	1 full cob of sweetcorn or ½ cup kernels
Sweet potato	½ small sweet potato
Tomatoes	1 medium tomato or 7 cherry tomatoes
Watercress	2 handfuls or 1 cup
Watermelon	⅙ small watermelon

How to use this book

The way we eat has changed significantly in the past 50 years or so. We no longer plan for the week, take time for a weekly Sunday roast or save fish for a Friday. Going back to this old-fashioned way of cooking is actually a great way of saving time and money, and it helps to avoid food waste, which is another huge issue that threatens our future food security. So, the way I've structured the recipes in this book hark back to an era gone-by, while also fitting in with our busy modern lives.

SPEND MORE, IT PAYS

Buying less meat enables you to spend more on better quality. Take more time choosing it, rather than just running to the supermarket to get whatever is on offer. Try to find a good butcher or farmers' market, or even better, a farm that delivers to you. There are plenty around and they need your support. Be wary of meat that doesn't have a farmer's name attached to it. Meat that's good for you has a story that wants to be told.

SUNDAY ROASTS

Each meat chapter begins with tips and recipes for making delicious and easy roast dinners. Roasting a large joint is lavish; it looks generous and you can really celebrate the seasons by serving it with a good selection of vegetables. As soon as you have a few good side dishes, you really only need a small slice of meat draped over the top of the plate to make the meal complete. It's the perfect way of eating less meat and more veg without feeling deprived.

EASY FOOD FOR THE WEEK

Enjoy your roasts sensibly and you'll be left with plenty of meat to see you through the rest of the week. This makes meal planning a breeze. It also economises energy on so many levels. If you have cooked meat in the fridge (it will keep for 4–5 days), throwing together a meal is a doddle, which means you're less likely to pick up a ready meal on your way home from work.

Each meat chapter has a selection of leftover recipes, labelled as 'Remains' in honour of my husband's Irish granny who used to call leftovers 'McShane's Remains'.

EATING FOR ONE

Even if you live on your own, there's no reason why you can't roast a whole chicken or half a leg of lamb once or twice a month. Invite friends or family over for dinner and freeze leftovers. Make some mini pies or soup; eat one during the week, pop two or three in the freezer.

You wouldn't do this every week, otherwise you'd end up with a very full freezer; but if you do this once a month, you'll be well stocked up for the weeks ahead.

HAVE FISH ON FRIDAYS

The fish section offers tips on buying sustainable fish, as well as many flexible recipes. If you're following the roast dinner ideas and meal plans, why not have fish on Friday? Fish is one of the fastest, healthiest foods there is, making it a great way to kick-start the weekend.

OTHER FAST FOODS

Soon after I'd started this project I had breakfast with a food editor of a national newspaper. I told him I was writing a recipe cookbook about eating less meat. He loved the idea but sighed and said that the joy of cooking with meat is that it's fast. You can just flash a steak in a pan and it's done. Vegetables take too long to cook, he moaned. Responding to his challenge, I've whipped up a whole chapter's worth of quick, 15-minute or less vegetable sides, soups and a great guide to making salads. There are also loads of meaty dishes that can be rustled up in less than 30 minutes.

5 A DAY

Every recipe in this book contributes to your 5 A Day, even the puddings. So, you really can have your cake and eat it.
Most of the recipes contain 2.5 portions of fruit and veg. Some contain a little bit less, while others contain more. On average, two recipes will give you your 5 A Day. But try to eat more than that. We should be eating *at least* five portions of fruit and veg, so pack in as many as you can. The picnic spread on pages 158–163 offers five portions. This meal illustrates how easy and delicious eating lots of healthy fruit and veg can be.

HEALTHY BREAKFASTS

Did you know that Kellogg's cereals were created in a bid for us to eat less meat? Sadly, now they don't really tick the box for optimal health as John Harvey Kellogg once intended. The 35g of sugar in a 100g bowl of Coco Pops is not my idea of a great start to the day. (That's more sugar than in a 100g bar of chocolate.) I've come up with a selection of easy, fruit-packed breakfasts to get you off on the right foot.

BEEF

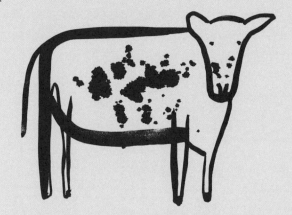

There are few things more delicious than a juicy steak or a meltingly tender forerib of beef with golden roast potatoes. Beef is a precious source of food and it can be extremely healthy, as well as environmentally friendly. Here's the key phrase: grass-fed.

When you opt for beef that comes from cattle that have been chomping on grass, all or at least most of the time, the shocking statistics about their detriment to the environment start to melt away. When cows aren't eating grass, they're fed grain. Growing grain is an enormous drain on resources, and it makes for unhealthy meat.

It takes 10kg of grain to produce just 1kg of beef. Because we eat so much beef, an enormous amount of grain needs to be grown. Nearly 40 per cent of the world's grain is fed to the animals we eat. If this grain was directly consumed by humans, it could adequately feed the 1.4 billion people who are living in dire poverty.

At the height of the same 1984 famine which inspired the historic Band Aid concert, Ethiopia was growing food to feed livestock in Britain and other European nations.

The strange thing is: cows should not eat grain. They don't have the enzymes to process it, certainly not in any great quantity. Acid builds up in the guts of cattle trying to digest grain, which can lead to ulcers and the formation of E. Coli along their digestive tract.

Why on earth would you feed cows grain if it causes so many problems? The answer: cows grow faster if you

In intensive farming systems, cows that used to grow to be four or five years old are now hurried to fatten up in just 14 months, and this is now being shortened to 11 months.

pump them full of grain. Time is money. If you can make more meat in less time, and encourage people to eat lots of it, you will have fat profits. A lot of the grain fed to these cows is subsidised (by taxpayers) and much of it is genetically modified. It's not a sustainable or healthy system.

Let's go to where the grass is actually greener. Happy cows that chew the cud grow a bit slower but their meat has up to four times as much heart-health improving and brain-boosting omega-3.

People who have ample amounts of omega-3s in their diet are less likely to have high blood pressure. They're also 50 per cent less likely to suffer a heart attack. Because omega-3s are essential for your brain as well, people who get a healthy dose decrease their risk of suffering from depression, schizophrenia, attention deficit disorder (ADD), or Alzheimer's disease.

Grass-fed beef has further health benefits: seven times as much beta-carotene and up to four times more vitamin E than grain-fed beef. It's also lower in calories and has a fat content on a par with that of a skinless chicken breast or wild deer.

A 6oz (175g) steak from a grass-fed cow can have 100 fewer calories than the grain-fed equivalent.

Letting cattle chomp grass is good for the environment, too. American cattleman Ridge Shinn in Hardwick, Massachusetts says 'Conventional cattle-raising is like mining. It's unsustainable, because you're just taking without putting anything back. But when you rotate cattle on grass, you change the equation. You put back more than you take.'

Cows and meat-eaters aren't villains when it comes to climate change. There is a lot of beautifully reared beef out there that is both in tune with nature and of benefit to our health. If you eat a portion less and spend a little bit more, you can savour the true value of beef.

1 BEEF RIB JOINT, 5 MEALS

THE MAIN EVENT

Roast rib of beef with roast
potatoes in dripping

Silky red wine gravy

Sticky orange-glazed shallots

Earthy cumin carrots

Broccoli with toasted almonds

Red cabbage braised in
balsamic vinegar

Pudding suggestion
Almond apple crumble

REMAINS

*Meals to get you through
the week*

Beefy Yorkshire puddings

Cold roast beef, beetroot and
watercress sandwich

Porcini bolognese

Beef in ginger miso broth

NOURISHING STOCK

Fresh beef bones
make for a richer
stock, but these
roasted bones will
also give you a
decent liqueur,
which you can use to
add flavour and a
nutritional boost to
your Beef in Ginger
Miso Broth and
Porcini Bolognese.
Once you've cooked
your roast, use the
bones within 3 days,
or freeze them for up
to 3 months.

FIRST QUARTER
Carve from the first quarter of the joint to serve up for your roast dinner. 50g is roughly the size of a 1–2cm-thick slice. If you fancy serving a little more meat, just trim back on the amount you use in one of the 'Remains' recipes.

SECOND QUARTER
You can't beat a **Cold Roast Beef Sandwich**. Meat from a joint you roasted yourself is so incredibly delicious and much nicer than any precooked sandwich meat. If you like your meat a little bit pink, carve from the second quarter nearing the centre. If you prefer your meat browner, use the fourth quarter, at the rear of the joint.

THIRD QUARTER
The centre of your roast is great for using in the **Ginger Miso Broth** because the warm broth allows you to cook the meat a bit further if it's too pink for your taste. Just simmer the broth until the meat is cooked to your liking.

FOURTH QUARTER AND FATTY BITS
The outside ends of a roasting joint always have the most flavour because this part of the flesh has been rubbed with spices and herbs and has caramelised in the heat of the oven. I like to use it in my **Porcini Bolognese** as you get a rich flavour without having to use heaps of beef. I also save any fatty bits that I've trimmed from the meat to fry up with the minced meat for added flavour.

LAYER OF FAT
The layer of fat beneath the crisped outside of the beef is great for rendering down and using to make **Yorkshire Puddings** and **Dripping Pastry**.

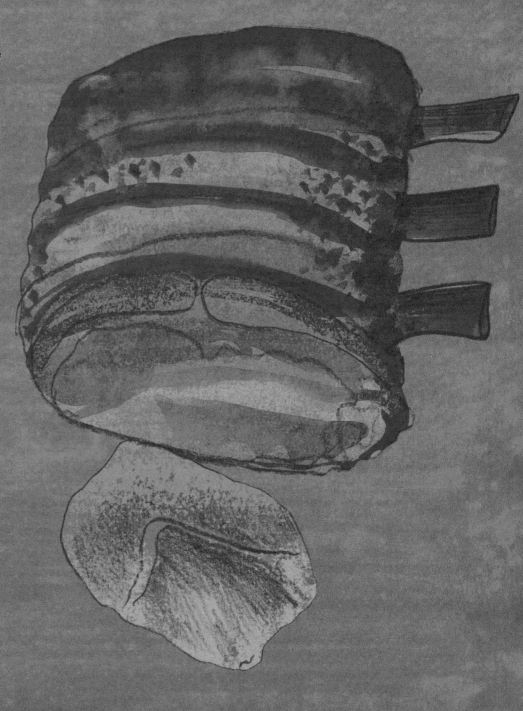

Roast rib of beef with roast potatoes in dripping

A forerib of beef is the ultimate roasting joint. It's slightly more expensive but you get so much more from it, such as bones for stock and a gorgeously crisp layer of fat on the top. It produces loads of dripping for your roast potatoes. As a bonus, there's also an extra layer of fat which you can melt down and use like butter for pastry or oil to fry chips.

Serve with three vegetable sides. See the Veg Patch chapter for recipe ideas.

SERVES 4, WITH ENOUGH LEFTOVERS FOR 3–4 MEALS FOR 4, PLUS STOCK AND FAT FOR EVEN MORE MEALS

4 large floury potatoes

1.5kg forerib joint of beef

leaves from a few sprigs of rosemary, finely chopped

3 garlic cloves, finely chopped

sea salt and freshly ground black pepper

If you can, parboil your potatoes in the morning, or an hour or so before you're ready to cook the beef. Peel, cut into chunky (roughly 3cm thick) hunks. (Save the peelings – you can fry them up to make delicious crisps to go with a cold roast beef sandwich the next day.) Place the potatoes in a roasting tin, in a single layer. Season and set aside in a dry, cool place.

Take the beef out of the fridge to get to room temperature. Preheat the oven to 230°C/gas mark 8.

Mix the garlic and rosemary with salt and pepper. Massage it into the beef, rubbing it into all the nooks and crannies. Place the beef in a snug roasting dish or tin — a large loaf tin or oval casserole dish works nicely.

Place the roasting tin on a middle rack in the oven and cook for 30 minutes, until the meat has a golden crust. Take the roasting tin out of the oven, spoon off the fat and pour it into the roasting tin with the potatoes. Turn the potatoes to coat them in the dripping. Place the beef back in the oven and set the potatoes alongside if possible or on the shelf below. Reduce the temperature to 160°C/gas mark 3 and cook for 1 hour 15 minutes. Check the potatoes a few times, giving the pan a shake to rotate them. Baste with extra dripping from the beef pan if needed.

Once cooked, remove the beef from the oven and let it rest for 30 minutes or more. If your potatoes are not quite there, take the meat out of the tin, crank the oven up to 220°C/gas mark 7 and pop the spuds back into the oven until golden.

While the beef relaxes, finish preparing the veg and make your gravy (see opposite).

Silky red wine gravy

Making amazing gravy couldn't be easier. All you need is the pan juices, some stock and a splash of decent wine (don't be afraid to use the good stuff, the better the wine, the better your gravy will be). The secret is to use good-quality ingredients.

500ml beef stock

300ml red wine

2 tablespoons balsamic vinegar

5 tablespoons pan juices

sea salt and freshly ground black pepper

Place the stock and red wine into a saucepan and bring to the boil. Reduce the liquid by a third. Stir in the balsamic vinegar and pan juices until well combined. Season to taste. Keep warm until ready to serve. Use any leftover gravy to make Porcini Bolognese (page 29) or drizzle over Beefy Yorkshire Puddings (page 25).

Beef stock

The bones from your roasting joint make a delicious pot of stock, which you can use in the Beef in Ginger Miso Broth and the Porcini Bolognese.

MAKES ABOUT 1 LITRE OF STOCK

beef bones leftover from Roast Rib of Beef (see opposite)

2 tablespoons olive oil or beef dripping

2 onions, quartered

2 large or 3 smaller carrots, halved lengthwise

2 large celery ribs, halved

1 bay leaf and/or a few sprigs of fresh thyme

a few black peppercorns (about 5)

100ml red wine (optional)

Place a pot over medium-high heat. Add the bones and the oil or beef dripping and let the bones sizzle for 5 minutes. Add the veg and bay leaf and let them fry for 10–15 minutes, until they start to pick up a bit of colour. Splash in the wine, if using, and let it reduce by half.

Pour in just enough water to cover and pop a lid on. Reduce the heat. Simmer for 2–3 hours, or overnight in a slow-cooker. Strain and decant into pots. To intensify the flavour of the stock (and save you space if you're freezer is full), you can reduce the stock down by half.

Cool and store in the fridge for 2 days, or freeze for up to 6 months.

Dripping

Once you've roasted your beef and start carving into it, you'll notice a soft, white layer of fat sitting just below the crisp, crackling-like top.

This bit is an amazing source for making a little pot of beef dripping. It's easy to make – all you have to do is melt it down in the oven, as outlined on the right.

This fat is extremely nutritious when it's from a well-reared, grass-fed piece of beef as it's loaded with healthy omega 3.

The dripping is ideal for making the Beefy Yorkshire Puddings, pastry or homemade chips.

Don't just limit your dripping-making skills to beef. Anytime you have excess fat on meat, be it a large roasting joint or a pork chop with a generous rind, just trim it off and melt it down. Dripping is a delicious alternative to butter and cooking oils.

TO RENDER FAT

Preheat the oven to 150°C/gas mark 2. Cut any fat remaining from your roast into 2cm hunks. Pop them into a small ovenproof pot, cover with a lid and cook for 1 hour.

Strain the fat using a fine mesh sieve, pressing the fat out of any nuggets that didn't fully melt down. The liquid should be clear.

Store in a jam jar for up to 1 month. You can re-use the fat up to 5 times – just strain until clear after use.

Beefy yorkshire puddings

Yorkshire puddings are outstanding when they're made with beef dripping. They also go down a treat as a stand-alone meal, especially when served with mash, gravy and two generous vegetable sides.

MAKES 12–16

110g plain flour

150ml milk

150ml water

2 eggs

1 tablespoon beef dripping for the batter, plus 10 teaspoons

a generous pinch of sea salt

2 OF YOUR 5 A DAY WHEN SERVED WITH TWO VEG SIDES

Preheat the oven to 220°C/gas mark 7. Bring the dripping to room temperature or melt in a saucepan.

Sift the flour into a large bowl. Whisk the milk, water, eggs and dripping together. Make a well in the centre of the flour and tip the liquid into the middle. Whisk until smooth and you get a few air bubbles into the batter.

Drizzle 1 teaspoon dripping into each hollow of a muffin tin. Place in the oven for 5 minutes, or until the oil is sizzling hot. Very carefully remove from the oven. Fill each hollow half-full with batter. Cook for 20–30 minutes, until risen and golden.

Dripping pastry

I normally get about 50g of rendered beef fat from a roast, which works perfectly in this recipe.

MAKES ENOUGH PASTRY FOR ONE LARGE PIE OR TART, OR 4–6 INDIVIDUAL ONES

45g cold beef dripping, scraped from the jar and roughly chopped into small pieces

125g plain white, stoneground flour

a good pinch of sea salt

2–3 tablespoons cold water

Put the chopped fat, flour and salt in a large bowl. Rub the fat into the flour until it resembles fine breadcrumbs. You can do this in a food processor if you like.

Sprinkle the water over 1 tablespoon at a time, until the flour mix starts to come together to form a not-too-soft but not-too-firm dough.

Dust the dough with flour and roll out if you're ready to use it. Roll on a floured surface until 5mm thick.

If not using the dough straight away, you can wrap it up and refrigerate it for up to 24 hours, or freeze it for up to 3 months.

If you're using the pastry for a tart, divide into two balls, line the tart case and bake blind in a 180°C/gas mark 4 oven for 10–15 minutes, until just browning. Cool and then fill your pastry and bake from there.

To add a pastry lid to a casserole or stew, simply roll out one of the balls of pastry. Place the cooled stew in a pie or baking dish. Carefully transfer the rolled pastry over the top of the dish.

Press the pastry around the sides of the dish to seal and tidy up or trim any stray bits. Gently prick the pastry a few times to allow steam to escape.

Brush the pastry with olive oil for a glossy finish. Bake until the pastry is golden – 30–45 minutes, depending on the size of your pie.

Cold roast beef, beetroot and watercress sandwich

A good sandwich should be seasoned and dressed like a salad: it keeps it succulent and adds layers of flavour. It also means you don't really need to butter the bread, though, to add an extra depth of meatiness, I've suggested adding a slick of warm, melted beef fat instead.

FOR EACH SANDWICH:

1–2 teaspoon-sized nuggets of fat trimmed from leftover roast

olive oil (optional)

2 slices from a good loaf of sourdough bread

dollop of horseradish or mustard (optional)

½ ripe avocado, thinly sliced

sea salt and black pepper

squeeze of lemon juice

a small handful of watercress

50g cold roast beef, thinly sliced

a little splash of balsamic vinegar

Sticky Orange-Glazed Shallots left over from the roast (see page 120), optional

2–3 slices cooked beetroot

❀ 2.5 OF YOUR 5 A DAY, MORE IF SERVED WITH CELERY AND CARROTS STICKS

To assemble: place a small frying pan over medium heat. Put the beef fat in the pan and heat until the fat has rendered out — the fat has tremendous flavour which is far more flavourful than butter. Press one side of each bread slice into the pan to mop up the fat, remembering that fat from a well-sourced piece of grass-fed beef is good for you – it's full of healthy omega 3s, vitamin E, etc.

Alternatively, brush a bit of olive oil on one side of each bread slice. Dab a bit of horseradish or mustard on as well, if you like.

Lay the avocado across one piece of bread. Season and add a squeeze of lemon juice. Pile the beef on and season. Splash a few drops of balsamic vinegar over it. Add the shallots, if using. Pile the beetroot slices on top followed by the watercress. Carefully place the slice of bread on the other and eat with joy!

POTATO PEELING CRISPS

Potato peelings make the most delicious crisps and are a great way to use every last scrap of the vegetable. They're also really easy to make. Pat dry or pop in the oven to remove some of their moisture, then shallow fry or roast in olive oil or beef dripping. Season and eat, or store in an airtight container for 2–3 days.

Porcini bolognese

This is an earthy version of a classic bolognese. It has less meat, yet more depth thanks to the hearty handful of porcini mushrooms and leftover roast beef. Make sure the meat you use has a good marbling of fat as this will add heaps of flavour.

SERVES 4

25g dried porcini mushrooms

150g leftover roast beef (about 3 1cm-thick slices), coarsely minced

125g fresh chestnut or portobello mushrooms, finely minced

sea salt and black pepper

350ml red wine

a few splashes of olive oil

2 onions, finely diced

4 large garlic cloves, chopped

2 large carrots, finely diced

2 sticks of celery, finely diced

800g tinned tomatoes

2 bay leaves

2 tablespoons tomato purée

250ml beef stock or leftover gravy (or a mix of both)

a few sprigs of rosemary and/ or thyme, leaves finely chopped

TO SERVE

400g dried spaghetti

a good handful of fresh rocket or watercress to serve

50g Parmesan cheese, finely grated

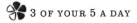 3 OF YOUR 5 A DAY

Pour enough boiling water over the dried porcini mushrooms to cover. Set aside to plump up for 10 minutes or so. Drain and finely chop.

Place a large pan or pot over a medium heat. Once hot, add the meat — no need for oil as there's enough fat in the meat. Fry until caramelised. Add the porcini and fresh mushrooms. Cook further, until take on some colour. Add a splash of olive oil at this point if needed, and season well. Tip into a clean dish and set aside.

Deglaze the pan with wine. Let it bubble up for a minute, then tip onto the dish with the meat.

Place the pan back on the heat. Add a splash of olive oil. Once warm, add the onions, garlic, carrots and celery. Season. Gently cook until it starts to pick up a bit of colour, about 25–30 minutes.

Once the veggies are soft, tip in the tomatoes and bay leaves, turn up the heat and let it bubble away for 5–10 minutes, until the tomato sauce has thickened. Stir in the tomato purée. Add the meat and mushroom mixture, along with the beef stock. Let it gently bubble for another 15–20 minutes, stirring occasionally. Stir in the fresh rosemary and let it simmer while you cook the pasta.

Serve the pasta with the sauce, a heap of watercress or rocket leaves on top, finished with a drizzle of olive oil and a small mound of Parmesan cheese.

Beef in ginger miso broth

The great thing about cooking with leftover roast beef is that you can always cook the pinker middle bits to your liking. So, if you're not a fan of rare meat, keep simmering the broth until the meat is just right for you.

SERVES 4

1.2 litres water or stock

4 small or 2 large carrots, cut into matchsticks

4cm piece of fresh ginger root, peeled and grated

2 garlic cloves, peeled and thinly sliced

100–200g leftover roast beef, cut into very thin strips

250g noodles (rice, wheat or soba — whatever you fancy)

2 tablespoons miso paste

8 spring onions or 1 leek, thinly sliced

300g baby spinach, kale, spring greens or pak choi

a handful of fresh basil, coriander, mint and/or chervil

1 red chilli, finely sliced, or a sprinkle of chilli flakes (optional)

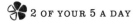 2 OF YOUR 5 A DAY

Place the stock, carrots, ginger and garlic in a saucepan. Pop a lid on and let it bubble away for 5 minutes. Add the beef and noodles. Simmer until the noodles are cooked through, about 5 minutes. Add the miso and stir until fully dissolved and incorporated. Fold in the spring onions and spinach until softened up. Serve with the herbs and chilli (if using) on top.

NOTE

If you don't have leftover roast beef, use a 100–200g steak, sliced into very thin strips. Add with the carrots, ginger and garlic.

Simple beef curry

Traditional Indian meals I've had feature one or two meat curries along with a myriad of vegetable sides. But it's difficult to create this kind of feast at home, so I've drawn all the vegetables and meat into this curry. It's beautifully balanced and easy to make.

SERVES 4

200g steak (rump works nicely here)

3 garlic cloves, peeled and chopped

sea salt and black pepper

1 large onion, finely chopped

400g sweet potatoes or seasonal squash, peeled and cubed

½ red or green chilli, deseeded and sliced

4 cloves

1 teaspoon garam masala

1 teaspoon ground coriander

1 teaspoon turmeric

1½ teaspoons ground cumin

400ml coconut milk

200g cherry or small plum tomatoes, halved

250g baby spinach

1 teaspoon lemon juice

olive oil

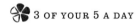 3 OF YOUR 5 A DAY

Rub a pinch of the garlic into the steak. Season and set aside. Heat a lidded pan over medium-high heat. Add a glug of oil. When warm, tumble in the onion and sweet potatoes or squash, and cook until softened and just starting to pick up colour, 5–10 minutes. Add the chilli and remaining garlic and cook for a further 2 minutes.

Fold in the spices and cook for a minute or two. Add the coconut milk and give it a stir. Cover and simmer for 20–30 minutes, until the sweet potatoes or squash are tender.

While it cooks, pan-fry the steak in a hot pan with a splash of olive oil. Cook for 3–4 minutes on each side until nicely coloured. Remove from the pan and let it rest for 10 minutes.

Thinly slice the meat and fold into the curry. Add the tomatoes and spinach, then cover and cook for a further 5 minutes. Finish with the lemon juice. Taste and adjust the seasoning, if needed. Serve with rice.

Cowboy-style braised beef
with pecan-dusted corn on the cob

*This is a hearty dish that was inspired by one of my favourite cookbooks,
A Cowboy in the Kitchen: Recipes from Reata and Texas West of the Pecos by
Grady Spears. I use a plump braising steak, instead of a whole pot-roasting
joint like he does, but it works a treat.*

SERVES 4

2 tablespoons plain white
flour

sea salt and black pepper

200g braising steak

olive oil

100ml ketchup

¼ teaspoon paprika

pinch of chilli powder

2 large carrots, peeled
and cut into chunky
rounds

2 large sweet potatoes,
peeled and cut into hunks

1 onion, peeled and
chopped

4 garlic cloves, peeled and
finely chopped

500ml beef stock

a handful of parsley and/
or coriander leaves,
roughly chopped

FOR THE CORN ON THE COB

4 whole sweetcorn cobs,
stripped of husks

100g pecan nuts, lightly
toasted

½ small garlic clove

a handful of coriander

olive oil

a pinch of sea salt

🍀 **THE STEW ALONE
OFFERS 2.5 OF YOUR 5 A
DAY, ADDING THE CORN
BUMPS IT UP TO 3.5**

Preheat the oven to 160°C/gas mark 3.

Season the flour and mix well. Coat the steak in the seasoned flour. Heat
the oil in an ovenproof casserole pot. Sear the steak for 3–4 minutes on
each side, until well browned. Add the ketchup, spices, carrots, sweet
potatoes, onions and garlic. Sweat for 5 minutes. Add the stock. Place in
the oven and cook for 2½ hours, until the beef is meltingly tender.

Boil the sweetcorn in a shallow bath of water until tender, 25–30
minutes. While it cooks, grind or finely chop the pecans, garlic and
coriander. Drain the sweetcorn, season and dust with the pecan mixture.

Serve the beef with a handful of herbs, sweetcorn and some wild rice.

Rosé veal parcels
with wild mushrooms and a plummy sauce

We've been conditioned not to buy veal because sometimes it's reared in cruel systems where the calves are kept in crates. However, a growing number of farmers are doing things differently. Their young cows frolic in grassy fields and have unlimited access to their mother's (or a stand-in cow's) milk. The meat they produce is healthier and pinker. Sometimes it's called 'rosé' veal. It's important to support these farmers. Veal, after all, is a by-product of the dairy industry.

SERVES 4

2 veal escalopes

1 leek, white and light green parts finely chopped

200g wild or chestnut mushrooms, finely chopped

3 garlic cloves, finely chopped

2 rosemary sprigs

200ml white wine

5 plums, halved and de-stoned

1 teaspoon honey

Sea salt and freshly ground pepper

🍀 2.5 OF YOUR 5 A DAY WHEN SERVED WITH ONE VEGETABLE SIDE

Halve the veal escalopes so that you have four square(ish) pieces of meat. Rub with olive oil and season. Set aside.

Remove the outer layer of your leek. Cut into long, 1cm-thick ribbons using kitchen scissors. You want 8–10 of these to tie up your veal parcels.

Place a frying pan over a high heat. Add a splash of olive oil. Sauté the mushrooms and leek until softened. Season. Add the garlic and cook for just a moment longer. Remove from the heat. Finely chop one of the rosemary sprigs. Fold through the mushrooms.

Pile a mound of the mushroom mixture into the centre of one of the veal pieces. Bring the sides up over the mixture to form a little parcel. Carefully tie it up with two leek ribbons. Repeat until you have four filled and tied parcels.

Place a large frying pan over a high heat and add a splash of oil. Gently place each of the parcels in the pan and cook for 2–3 minutes on each side, until nicely browned. Pour the wine over them and let it bubble up for a minute.

Place the parcels on a plate. Add the plums to the pan, along with the remaining rosemary sprig and honey. Cook at a soft rolling boil until the wine has reduced a bit and the plums start to soften.

Dot two plums on each plate, leaving two in the pan. Turn the heat to high and let the sauce thicken up, mashing the remaining plums into the sauce until they start to melt into it. Strain the sauce and pour over the parcels.

Serve with boiled new potatoes or mash and a green vegetable side.

Maya Gold chilli

This recipe's from a good friend, Tina, and her husband Ian. Their chilli is rich and voluptuous, with loads of earthy spice and a hint of chocolate.

You can use any dark chocolate but Green & Black's Maya Gold gives the best results. It has a hint of orange and a medley of spices including cinnamon, vanilla and nutmeg that lift the dish to new heights. When you have all this going on you really don't clock the fact that there's less meat in the chilli. Add a little grating of orange zest along with the chocolate if it's not Maya Gold.

SERVES 6

olive oil

1 medium onion, finely chopped

2 bell peppers (any colour or a mix), sliced into 2cm chunks

3 garlic cloves, finely chopped

250g minced beef, venison or buffalo

1 tablespoon each ground cinnamon, paprika and cumin

800g tinned tomatoes

30g Green & Black's Maya Gold dark chocolate, broken into pieces

1 teaspoon brown sugar

1 tablespoon tomato purée

a pinch of chilli powder, to taste

400g tinned kidney beans, drained

400g tinned black beans, drained

TO SERVE

50g natural yogurt, crème fraîche or sour cream

a handful of fresh coriander

lime

paprika

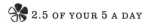 2.5 OF YOUR 5 A DAY

Place a pot over a medium heat and add a splash of oil. Sizzle the onion, peppers and garlic until they start to soften, but not fry, for about 20 minutes. Add the meat to the pan and cook to seal and colour for a couple of minutes. Fold in the spices and let them cook into the meat for a few minutes. Add the tinned tomatoes.

Let it bubble up for a bit, then stir in the chocolate, brown sugar and tomato purée. Taste and add a dash of chilli, if you like (or you can stir into individual bowls when you serve). Fold in the kidney and black beans. Turn the heat right down and simmer for an hour or so, stirring occasionally to prevent burning.

Serve with yogurt, coriander and lime or just yogurt sprinkled with paprika. It's delicious with rice or over jacket potatoes. In the autumn, try serving your chilli in a pumpkin bowl (see below).

PUMPKIN BOWLS

This is a stunning way to serve chilli and it gives you another portion of veg.

Cut the top off a pumpkin. Scoop the seeds out. Roast it whole until the flesh is tender — 20-30 minutes at 200°C/gas mark 6 for small pumpkins, 45 minutes to 1 hour for a larger one. Once tender, spoon the warm chilli inside and serve.

Or, if you're reheating the chilli, place the cold chilli in a hollowed, uncooked pumpkin and roast, replacing the lid, until the pumpkin is tender and the chilli warmed through, about 45 minutes. Scoop the pumpkin flesh out with your spoon as you eat/serve the chilli.

Carpaccio with a Venetian salad

I love this dish because it really illustrates how you can have a beautiful and bold plate of food, while striking a harmonious balance between meat and veg. When I served this to my husband he remarked: 'Are you really allowed to have that much meat?'

SERVES 4

200g fillet steak

olive oil

sea salt and black pepper

FOR THE VENETIAN SALAD

3-4 small cooked beetroot or 2 larger ones

4-6 baby courgettes or 1 large courgette

juice and zest of 1 lemon

sea salt and black pepper

olive oil

1 large or 2 small avocados

8 marinated artichoke hearts

a large handful of wild rocket

a handful of toasted pine nuts

✿ WITH THE SALAD IT GIVES YOU 2.5 OF YOUR 5 A DAY

There are two ways to make this: slicing or pounding.

Slicing can be done with a long and nicely sharpened knife and works best when the meat is nearly frozen. So, either pop it into the freezer for an hour or two before carving, or defrost for an hour or so and then slice. It's best to use a larger piece of fillet for this, just so you have something to hold on to as you slice the meat. Save the unused piece for kebabs (page 62) or homemade burgers (page 41). If you're slicing, 50g meat should give you 3-4 slices, enough to cover a plate.

Pounding is easier and is the method we used when I was a chef at Quo Vadis, in London's Soho. Slice the beef into 50g hunks, going against the grain, just as if you were slicing small fillet steaks. Place between two big sheets of clingflim or parchment paper and use a meat hammer to pound it as thinly as you can without tearing the meat. Smooth it out through the paper/clingfilm and then remove the top piece. Place a plate over the top and flip the steak onto it, very gently removing the bottom film/paper. Drizzle with olive oil and season.

To assemble the salad, cut the beetroot into chunky, bite-sized pieces. Halve or quarter the baby courgettes or slice a large courgette into nuggets. Squeeze a bit of lemon juice over the courgettes, season and then fry in a splash of olive oil, just until they've picked up a bit of colour. Set aside to cool. Peel and slice the avocado. Halve the artichoke hearts. Gently combine the veggies. Season and grate some lemon zest over. Squeeze the remaining lemon juice over and drizzle with olive oil. Fold in the rocket and pine nuts.

Serve the carpaccio with a mound of the salad in the middle.

NOTE If you want to add extra depth of flavour, roll the edges of the beef in spices before pounding or slicing. A blend of coarsely ground cumin and coriander, along with some garlic, is nice.

Ranch-hand steak salad with chimichurri sauce

One of the key tricks I've learned in creating all these recipes is that when you're using less meat, you need to add a bold kick of flavour to bring back the oomph. Here, I've done it in two places.

In the BBQ section of the book you'll find a coffee rub – this takes seconds to make. If you massage a bit of it into your steak, it deepens its rich, meaty taste. The chimichurri sauce - which is also easy to whip up – lifts the whole thing up and makes it sing. This is a marvellous dish. I beg you to try it.

SERVES 4

FOR THE SALAD

2 red peppers

4 corn on the cob

head of a crisp lettuce or a few handfuls of salad leaves

1 red onion, peeled, halved and sliced (about 1cm thick)

a splash of olive oil

2 avocados

FOR THE STEAK

1 x 200g sirloin or rib-eye steak

Coffee Rub, see page 64

FOR THE CHIMICHURRI

100ml olive oil

1½ tablespoons red wine vinegar (or red wine)

grated zest of 1 lemon plus 1 tablespoon juice

1 large garlic clove, finely chopped

1 shallot or small onion, peeled and quartered

½ teaspoon sea salt

¼ teaspoon black pepper

a thick slice of red chilli, finely chopped

50g fresh mixed herbs (parsley, coriander and mint work well), roughly chopped

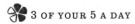 3 OF YOUR 5 A DAY

Preheat the oven to 220°C /gas mark 7, or fire up the grill.

Place the peppers, corn cobs and onions on a baking tray with a splash of olive oil. Roast until the peppers are lightly charred, the corn is tender and starting to colour and the onions are soft and starting to caramelise. This will take 30–40 minutes.

While the vegetables cook, massage the Coffee Rub into the steak and let the meat warm up to room temperature.

Make the chimichurri by placing all the ingredients in a blender, apart from the herbs. Blitz until the onion is chopped and the mixture looks a bit creamy. Add the herbs in three batches until they're well combined.

As soon as the veg are done, remove from the heat and flash the steak into the oven or on the grill. Cook for 3–5 minutes on each side, depending on how well done you like it and how thick your steak is.

Carefully pull the skin from the pepper and tear the pepper into ribbons, scraping the seeds out as you go along. Arrange the ribbons on plates. Top with salad leaves. Divide the onion slices among the plates. Slice and add the avocado. Slice the steak and divide among the plates. Pop a corn cob on the side of each plate, like a wedge of bread sitting next to a bowl of soup. Drizzle a good bit of chimichurri over the steak and serve.

3 great burgers

Burgers are the ultimate pin-up for meat eaters. They're also, funny enough, great vehicles for vegetables. My mother taught me this trick. She always adds a hearty handful of chopped onions and peppers for added moisture and flavour. Inspired by this technique, I've created three quite different, but equally delicious, burgers that have a brilliantly tasty blend of meat and veg.

How to make your own mince

Making your own mince is ridiculously simple — and you don't need a fancy mincer. It's a great way to use scraps of meat left over from other dishes. I tend to have a burger fest at the end of the month when I'm clearing the freezer. Meat is easier to mince up when it's partially frozen, so this works nicely.

BEEF CUTS

You can mince virtually any cut for your burger. Rump, fillet, sirloin and rib-eye steaks work nicely. You can also buy a silverside or topside roasting joint and use a hunk of it in one of the stew recipes, saving the remaining bits for burgers or kebabs. A braising steak will also work, as long as you trim out any sinewy bits. The perfect burger would include a little nugget of fat chopped up with the meat.

LAMB

Lamb, hogget and mutton make wonderful burgers. Use neck fillet, the meat from chops or cutlets (carve the meat away from the bones and use the bones for soup or stock), chump steaks, or you can use a slice carved off the end of a roasting joint (leg or shoulder).

PORK

You can mince any cut of pork: chops, escalopes, a slice from a pork loin roasting joint. The key is to get your fat ratio right. If you're mincing a pork chop, trim off some of the fatty rind to mince up with the meat. Render any excess fat down (see page 25) or roast it to make crackling.

TO MINCE

Chop the meat using a fairly large, heavy knife, or cut it into nuggets – you'll be able to mince it more finely if the meat is partially frozen. Make sure you include a bit of fat – this keeps your burgers moist and helps them to stick together. It also adds heaps of flavour. Lean fat typically has 10 per cent fat. To emulate this, you should add a teaspoon-sized nugget of fat for every 50g meat. Once you've finely chopped your meat and fat, you can pulse in a food-processor to mince it further, if you like.

Mushroom burgers with Asian slaw

You'll find a lot of mushrooms in this book. That's because their texture and flavour are very similar to those of meat, especially beef. Ground up finely like mince, they work stunningly. I love this burger. The splash of soy and the bite of fresh ginger just make them out of this world.

I like sticking with the Asian theme by serving these burger patties wrapped up in a pak choi leaf, but my husband prefers them in a burger bun.

SERVES 4

250g chestnut or portobello mushrooms, roughly chopped

200g beef or buffalo mince

6 spring onions, finely chopped

2 garlic cloves, finely chopped

3cm piece of fresh ginger, peeled and grated

2 tablespoons soy sauce

3 tablespoons sesame seeds, toasted

sea salt and black pepper

a splash of olive oil

8 pak choi, green cabbage or large lettuce leaves

FOR THE ASIAN SLAW

½ white, green or red cabbage, shredded

2 carrots, cut into matchsticks

a few large handfuls of fresh coriander leaves, roughly chopped

100g cashew nuts, toasted

1 tablespoon honey

2 tablespoons fresh lime juice

1 tablespoon apple cider, white wine or rice vinegar

1 tablespoon sesame oil

½ tablespoon soy sauce

2cm piece of fresh ginger, peeled and grated

2.5 OF YOUR 5 A DAY

Put the chopped mushrooms in a food-processor and pulse until they reach a mince-like consistency.

Tip them into a bowl with the beef or buffalo mince, spring onions, garlic, ginger, soy sauce and sesame seeds. Season. Mix well and form into four patties. Pop them into the fridge to firm up for at least 10 minutes and up to 3 hours.

Make the Asian Slaw while you wait. Mix the cabbage, carrots, coriander and toasted cashew nuts.

Whisk the honey, lime juice, vinegar, sesame oil, soy sauce and ginger together. Pour over the slaw, mix well and refrigerate until ready to use.

Heat a large frying pan over medium-high heat. Add a splash of olive oil. Cook the burgers until golden and cooked through, about 5–7 minutes on each side.

Serve each burger wrapped in pak choi, cabbage or lettuce leaves, alongside a mound of the Asian slaw.

VARIATION
Apple Beetroot Slaw Omit the carrots and add matchsticks of 1 apple and 1 raw beetroot to the slaw.

Pork, apricot and fennel burgers

These burgers are great as they deliver a good heap of veg before you've even draped a lettuce leaf over them, and the vegetables are not there as a gimmick. The finely minced fennel and onion keep these pork burgers deliciously moist.

MAKES 4 BURGERS

6 dried apricots, finely chopped

½ fennel, roughly chopped

½ onion, roughly chopped

2 garlic cloves, peeled

2 tablespoons pine nuts, toasted

200g minced pork

a little finely chopped chilli (optional)

a handful of tarragon, parsley or mint, finely chopped

sea salt and freshly ground pepper

a splash of olive oil

TO SERVE

4 burger buns

a few crisp lettuce leaves

2 OF YOUR 5 A DAY

Preheat oven to 180°C/gas mark 6.

Place the apricots, fennel, onion, garlic and pine nuts in a food processor. Blend until finely minced.

Combine this mixture with the minced pork, chilli (if using) and the herbs. Season well. Divide the mixture into four and shape into burger patties, squeezing out any excess moisture.

Place an oven-proof frying pan over medium heat and add a splash of olive oil. Carefully transfer the burger patties to the pan. Sizzle for a few minutes. Gently flip the burgers, pressing them back into shape, if needed. Place the pan in the oven to finish cooking for 20–25 minutes. Roasting the burgers this way helps them cook through. Check one of the burgers by inserting a knife into the centre, and checking to make sure the meat looks more white than rosy. If so, they're done.

Serve the burgers in a bun with crispy salad leaves, shaved fennel and a dab of chilli jam, or your favourite condiment.

Lamb burger
with roasted aubergine and pistachio mayonnaise

Aubergines have a hearty, meaty texture and work beautifully with lamb,
especially when they've developed a smoky flavour after roasting.

MAKES 4 BURGERS

1 aubergine

olive oil

sea salt and freshly
ground black pepper

2 large garlic cloves,
finely chopped

2 red peppers

200g minced lamb

1 onion, finely chopped

½ teaspoon each ground
cumin, ground coriander
and ground cinnamon

10 cardamom pods, seeds
ground

pinch of chilli powder

4 tablespoons
breadcrumbs

3 tablespoons black olives,
finely chopped

a handful of fresh mint

4 nice bread rolls, halved
and brushed with olive oil

a handful of salad or
lettuce leaves

FOR THE PISTACHIO MAYO

3 tablespoons shelled
pistachios, lightly toasted

sea salt and black pepper

zest and juice of 1 lemon

1 ripe avocado, flesh
scooped out

¼ teaspoon honey

3 tablespoons olive oil

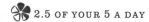 2.5 OF YOUR 5 A DAY

Preheat the oven to 200°C/gas mark 6. Halve the aubergine and rub the insides with olive oil, a pinch of salt and half the garlic. Make three or four diagonal slices, about 1–2cm deep, across the flesh of each aubergine half. Do the same in the opposite direction. Grind a bit of pepper over the top, place on a roasting tray and pop into the oven for about 30 minutes, or until really tender right the way through. Add the whole red peppers in a tray alongside the aubergine.

Once cooked, set the peppers aside to cool, and put the aubergines in a blender and whizz to a fine purée, or finely chop them, skin and all, until you have a fairly fine paste. You can do this a day in advance if you're feeling organised.

Add the chopped aubergine to the lamb mince along with the onion, spices, breadcrumbs, chopped olives, remaining garlic and mint. Mix thoroughly and shape into four patties.

Let the burger patties rest while you make the Pistachio Mayo. To make it, blitz the pistachios in a food-processor or pound with a pestle in a mortar, with a pinch of salt, until you have a smooth, peanut butter-like paste. Add the avocado, honey and oil, and whizz until smooth and creamy. Taste and add more salt and pepper, if needed. Drizzle some olive oil over the top. Refrigerate until needed.

Prepare the red pepper by tearing it into 1cm-thick ribbons, removing skin, seeds and stem. Set aside.

Heat a frying pan over a medium-high heat. Add a splash of oil, let it warm, then carefully place the burger patties in the pan. Cook for 5 minutes, or until nicely browned on each side. If needed, press the burgers back into shape as they cook.

As soon as they're cooked, pile them into the dry burger buns to rest. The buns will act like little sponges to soak up all those lovely juices.

Serve the burgers with a dab of the Pistachio Mayo, the roasted red pepper ribbons and a handful of leaves.

LAMB

Some ecologists believe livestock provide the biodiversity that trees on their own cannot. According to Simon Fairlie, 'they are the best means we have of keeping wide areas clear and open to solar energy and wind energy.'

Rearing animals sustainably for meat plays an important role in shaping our ecosystem, argues former vegan Simon Fairlie in his book *Meat: A Benign Extravagance*. Sheep offer a great example of this. They thrive in some of the wildest, most wind-swept landscapes, where other food cannot be grown. Sheep tend not to be intensively farmed, but forage for grass, wildflowers and herbs. Their hillside grazing helps to limit hostile bracken and scrub, creating suitable habitats for other flora and fauna. People who rear sheep are usually called 'hill farmers' because of their vital contribution in stewarding these rugged terrains.

In Britain, the hilly uplands provide 70 per cent of the country's drinking water and they store billions of tonnes of carbon in deep peat bogs. The moorland managed by sheep farmers Nelly and Phillip Trevelyan of Hill Top Farm in North Yorkshire is said to lock in more carbon than all the forests of Britain and France put together.

If these hills were left to go wild, these virtues would crumble because grasslands act as sinks for carbon. Grazing sheep on the hills keeps the land grassy. This applies to areas in Australia, New Zealand and the US too.

Alas, the livelihood of these important farmers is at risk. Money is the problem. The culture of cheap food and meat has made it difficult for these farmers to even cover their costs. As a result, many hill farmers are giving up.

What can you do to preserve and enjoy this sustainable source of meat? The happy answer is: lots! For a start, buy traditionally reared lamb, hogget and mutton (more on those below) directly from a farmer. Many have their own websites and will deliver meat directly to your home, or you can find them at farmers' markets. If you buy lamb from a supermarket or butcher, ask them where it's farmed and how.

Secondly, eat lamb when it's in season. Although you can buy lamb year-round, the healthiest and most traditionally reared meat comes to market later on in the year.

Ewes typically lamb around Easter. The best are reared for around six months. This gives them plenty of time to spend with their mothers and then be weaned on lush summer grass. This is why it's best to buy lamb from early autumn through winter.

Even better, seek out hogget or mutton. Hogget comes from young sheep that have even longer lives. They live between 12 and 24 months. Mutton comes from animals that are still youthful, at 24 to 36 months.

The meat from mutton and hogget can be just as succulent and tender as lamb. The added benefit, beyond giving these animals longer, richer lives, is that they've had more time to graze, making their meat much tastier. In blind tastings, mutton often wins out to lamb.

When buying lamb, ask how long it was hung. The best meat will have a good layering of fat, allowing it to be hung for one to two weeks, creating flavoursome meat.

Most hill farmers actually prefer the taste of mutton over lamb.

1 LEG OF LAMB, 5 MEALS

THE MAIN EVENT

Roast leg of lamb with
pan-roasted garlic potatoes
PAGE 52

Fresh mint sauce
PAGE 52

Earthy cumin carrots
PAGE 118

Sweet balsamic beetroot
with a hint of chilli
PAGE 116

Lemony courgettes with
pine nuts
PAGE 118

Pudding suggestion
Mexican chocolate mousse
PAGE 209

REMAINS

*Meals to get you through
the week*

Roast lamb pitas with
baba ghanoush
PAGE 55

Shepherd's pie
PAGE 54

Beetroot, pea and
watercress salad
PAGE 53

Irish barley broth
PAGE 57

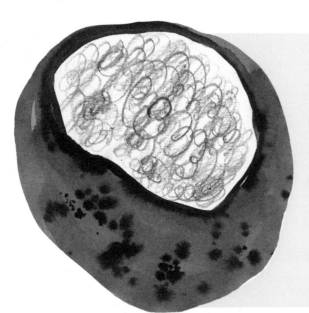

EXTRA USE FOR YOUR DRIPPING

If you place a layer of sliced potatoes
beneath your lamb, they'll do a marvellous
job of mopping up all the delicious, meaty
juices. But you should still have a good few
spoonfuls left lingering in the pan.

Use these juices instead of butter to flavour
a mash for your Shepherd's Pie.

To save you time, roast whole baking
potatoes alongside your lamb, scoop out the
flesh, mash with the pan juices and you'll
have an instant mash ready for your pie.

MEATY END OF THE LEG

Carve from the first quarter of the joint for your roast dinner. Two or three thin slices, depending on how thin you carve, is roughly what you'll need if you're serving the meal with potatoes and three vegetable sides.

MOVING TOWARD THE CENTRE

Cut a few thin slices to top off the **Roast Lamb Pitas with Baba Ghanoush**. This is a great meal to have the night after your roast dinner. To save time and conserve energy, roast an aubergine in the oven while you're roasting the lamb. You'll then have everything ready to go for a super-fast and healthy weeknight supper.

FAT AND MEAT CLOSER TO THE BONE

After you've carved a good few slices from your leg of lamb, the meat on offer narrows and is closer to the bone. This harder-to-get-at meat is great for making **Shepherd's Pie**. Just pull or roughly carve 175g (about a coffee mug full) of meat, including some fat, and mince it in a food-processor or using a good knife.

THE BONE AND ANY REMAINAING MEAT

The **Irish Barley Broth** is a great dish as it makes a stock and a hearty soup at the same time. Just pop the bone in the pot with the veggies, barley and any leftover scraps of meat and let it simmer away. The broth can also be made in a slow cooker, if you have one. Freeze the bone and any leftover meat if you want to save making this dish for a rainy day.

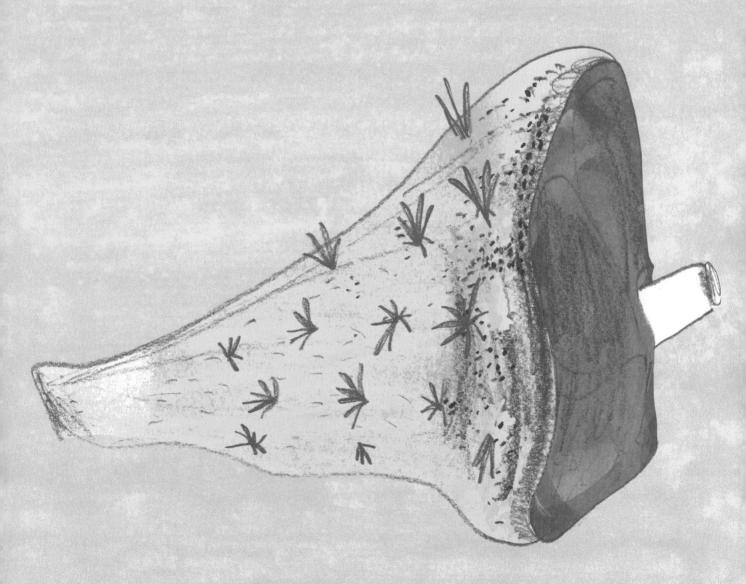

Roast leg of lamb
with pan-roasted garlic potatoes and fresh mint sauce

I once met a farmer who said he wouldn't sell his meat off the bone. I see his point. It's extra work for him and the bone adds so much flavour, so why remove it? It's also extremely nourishing – once you've carved most of the meat, toss it in a pot and make a soul-warming Irish barley broth, see page 57.

SERVES 4, WITH ENOUGH LEFTOVERS FOR 3-4 MEALS

1kg new potatoes or a small variety (regular spuds will also do)

½ lemon, quartered

a few sprigs of rosemary

4 garlic cloves, peeled

1.5kg half leg of lamb, bone-in

olive oil

sea salt and black pepper

FOR THE FRESH MINT SAUCE

2 large handfuls of fresh mint leaves, finely chopped

2 tablespoons cider vinegar

2 tablespoons apple juice

1 tablespoons caster sugar

Preheat the oven to 220°C/gas mark 7.

Scrub your potatoes clean and pat dry. Cut into 1cm slices, leaving the skin on. Scatter over the bottom of the roasting tray. It's OK if they overlap a bit, just make sure they're not piled too high.

Nestle the lemon pieces in among the potatoes. Tuck a few sprigs of rosemary in there. Halve two of the garlic cloves and add them to the potatoes.

Place the lamb on top of the potatoes. Rub a bit of olive oil, salt and pepper into it. Use a small, pointy knife to make a few 1–2cm pricks all over the meat. Thinly slice the remaining garlic clove and push the slices into the holes you've just made. Add a bit of rosemary as well.

Pop into the oven for a 30-minute sizzle – this helps the lamb develop a golden crust. Then reduce the temperature to 160°C/gas mark 3. Give the potatoes a good mix, to ensure they cook evenly. Return the roasting tray to the oven and cook for 1 hour. Remove the lamb from the tray and let it rest on a platter until ready to serve (don't worry, it will stay warm for a good while).

Return the potatoes to the oven to finish cooking, if needed. Make up the mint sauce by mixing all the ingredients together, and set aside while you make the vegetable side dishes.

Beetroot, pea and watercress salad

This salad has so many flavours and textures going on that the added slivers of roast lamb are like the icing on top.

SERVES 4

2 beetroot, cut into 2cm wedges

a few glugs of olive oil

a drizzle of honey

300g frozen peas

100g watercress

juice and zest of ½ lemon

leftover potatoes from your roast or boiled new potatoes

125g cold roast lamb, chopped

75g natural or Greek yogurt

1 garlic clove, finely minced

4 tablespoons grated cucumber

a few fresh mint leaves

 2.5 OF YOUR 5 A DAY

Splash some olive oil into a large frying pan. Add the beetroot and sauté until tender, 10–15 minutes. Drizzle the honey over. Set aside to cool.

Place the peas in a colander and rinse in warm water until defrosted.

Divide the watercress between the plates. Season with salt and pepper, drizzle the lemon juice and olive oil over, scatter with lemon zest and toss to combine. Set the beetroot pieces among the watercress, then add the potatoes. Sprinkle the peas over the top. Gently mix through the watercress leaves. Dot the lamb over the top.

For the dressing, mix the yogurt with the garlic, cucumber and mint, and season to taste. Drizzle this over the top of the salad and serve.

Shepherd's pie from leftover roast lamb

The key to making an outstanding shepherd's pie is to use meat from a leftover roast. It lends a richness you just can't get from a packet of mince. I've also added extra depth by suggesting that you fold dripping from your roast lamb through the mashed potato topping. Then, to finish it all off, a few pats of butter melting over the top of the mash just before serving.

SERVES 4

olive oil or lamb dripping from your roast

1 large onion, peeled and finely chopped

2 carrots, peeled and finely diced

2 sticks celery, finely diced

2 leeks, white and light green parts, finely chopped

2 large garlic cloves, peeled and finely chopped

175g (about 2 fistfuls) leftover roast lamb (make sure you include about 1 tablespoon of the fatty bits)

150ml lamb or veg stock, or broth leftover from Irish Barley Broth (page 57)

8 sprigs of thyme, leaves only

1½ tablespoons tomato purée

250ml red wine

1kg mashed potatoes

2 tablespoons butter

sea salt and freshly ground black pepper

🍀 1.5 OF YOUR 5 A DAY, 2.5 WITH A VEGETABLE SIDE

Place a large frying pan or pot over medium-high heat. Add enough olive oil or lamb dripping to finely coat the bottom of the pan. When heated, add the onions, carrots, celery, leeks and garlic, and sauté until softened.

Roughly chop the lamb. Place in a food-processor and grind to a fine mince (so it looks a bit like bought mince). Make sure you have some fatty bits in there — it will add heaps of flavour – but make sure that the fat is properly ground up.

Add the minced lamb to the veg and cook until it starts to really brown, to the point where it's starting to catch on the bottom of the pan, but not too much!

Drizzle with the stock or broth, just enough to wet the mixture. Season. Once all the vegetables have softened up, stir in the tomato purée. Let it cook for a minute, then pour in the wine. Let it reduce enough to give the meat and vegetables a glossy coating. Fold in the thyme. Tip this mixture into a baking dish (something large enough to hold four hearty portions).

Top with the mash. Drizzle or brush a tiny bit of olive oil over the top. Place a baking tray, foil or something ovenproof over the mash to keep it from burning. Bake for 30 minutes at 180°C/gas mark 4. Remove the tray or foil covering the mash and let it cook uncovered for 15 minutes.

Slice the butter into fine slivers and dot over the mash. Serve with a side of steamed broccoli.

Roast lamb pitas with baba ghanoush

Baba ghanoush is a dip made out of roasted or barbecued aubergines and it goes beautifully with lamb. Dollop a bit into a warmed pita bread, top with a few tomato and cucumber slices, or other veg, and finish with slices of cold roast lamb. Roast the aubergine alongside your lamb to save you time and your oven energy.

SERVES 4

FOR THE BABA GHANOUSH

1 aubergine

1 garlic clove, finely minced

2 teaspoons tahini (sesame seed paste)

sea salt

juice and zest of 1 lemon

olive oil

ground cumin or paprika, to garnish (optional)

TO GO WITH IT

200g leftover roast lamb

4–8 pita breads, lightly toasted

fresh tomatoes

cucumber, sliced or cut into fingers

avocado slices

radishes

carrots, grated or cut into fingers

black olives

crisp salad leaves

fresh mint, coriander and/or parsley

lemon wedges

olive oil

2.5 OF YOUR 5 A DAY

Preheat oven to 200°C/gas mark 6.

Halve the aubergine lengthwise. Brush with oil and cut diagonal, 1cm-deep lines across the flesh of each half. Repeat in the opposite direction, giving it a crisscrossed look. Roast in the oven for 30 minutes or until fully softened.

Place the aubergine halves in the food-processor and whizz with the garlic into a smooth purée. Mix with the tahini, lemon juice, a good pinch of salt and pepper and enough oil to bring it together and give it a smooth, glossy texture (roughly 2–3 tablespoons). Sprinkle a bit of spice over the top, if using, before serving.

Spoon the baba ghanoush into a bowl and serve it on a large wooden cutting board alongside cold slices of leftover lamb, warm pita bread and a good selection of vegetables. You can then fill the pitas with a dab of the aubergine dip, some lamb and a bit of veg. Snack on any vegetables that won't fit inside the breads, mopping up the baba ghanoush as you go along.

Irish barley broth

This is a great way to use up the last of the meat and bone from your leg of lamb. It requires slow cooking but this draws out all the flavour and nutrition from the lamb bone.

SERVES 4

a few glugs of olive oil

2 onions, peeled and chopped

200g leftover lamb, cut into chunky cubes

bone from leg of lamb (optional)

2 large carrots, peeled and cubed

350g root vegetables (swede, parsnips, celeriac and/or Jerusalem artichokes), peeled and cubed

2 large garlic cloves, peeled and finely chopped

sea salt and freshly ground pepper

4 large sprigs of thyme

6 tablespoons pearl or pot barley

1½ tablespoons cider vinegar or Worcestershire sauce

2 handfuls of parsley, chervil, kale or any other green you can finely chop and add for a healthy kick of colour

2.5 OF YOUR 5 A DAY

Place a large pot over medium-high heat. Add enough olive oil to coat the bottom. Once the oil is warm, add the onions and cook until golden.

Add the lamb, the lamb bone, if using, and the carrots. Cook until the carrots have started to soften, about 8 minutes or so. Add the other root veg and the garlic and let them sweat down a bit.

Add a splash of olive oil, if needed. Once the root veg have softened, add the thyme and barley. Let the barley toast for a moment. Add a good grinding of pepper.

Pour in enough water to just cover everything. Pop a lid on and let it bubble away over low heat for 1 hour.

Once cooked, stir through the vinegar or Worcestershire sauce. Taste and add a pinch of salt, if needed. Chop the herbs or greenery. Chuck them into the pot but don't stir them in. Spoon the soup into bowls, ensuring each person gets a good portion of greens on top.

Quick lamb cutlets or chops
with an autumnal grape and fig sauce

Spring lamb is a classic menu item but the best-tasting lamb is actually born in the spring. By the time it's mature, the leaves are starting to change, wine makers are plucking their grapes, and figs are ripening on the trees, making this dish a seasonal match made in heaven. For even richer, more delicious flavours, opt for hogget or mutton instead of lamb.

SERVES 4

sea salt and black pepper

a splash of olive oil

4 lamb cutlets or chops, seasoned with salt and pepper

250g grapes, preferably red but green will work nicely as well, halved

6 figs (dried or fresh), thinly sliced

350ml red wine

1 tablespoon honey

a sprig of rosemary

a few fresh mint leaves (about 8)

3 OF YOUR 5 A DAY WHEN SERVED WITH SQUASH OR WHITE BEAN MASH

Season the lamb with salt and pepper. Place a large frying pan over medium-high heat. Add a splash of olive oil. When warm, add the seasoned lamb cutlets or chops. Fry for 3–5 minutes on each side, giving the meat a golden crust. Prop each chop up so the fatty rind can fry on its side until golden, 2–3 minutes.

Remove the lamb from the pan and place on the plates.

Add the grapes and figs to the hot pan. Lower the heat a bit and stir the fruit in the fat for a minute. Pour in the wine and let it bubble up. Stir in the honey and let it gently bubble until reduced by half. Sprinkle the rosemary and mint over and serve.

These taste delicious with Autumn Squash and Sage Mash or Creamy Cannellini Mash (see page 128).

QUICK STOCK MADE FROM LEFTOVER BONES

Don't chuck out the bones left from your eaten chops or cutlets. Strip any leftover meat off. Place the bones in a pot with a splash of olive oil. Let them sizzle for a moment.

Add a quartered onion, two halved carrots, a bay leaf and/or a few sprigs of thyme and a few peppercorns. Fry the veg and bones for a moment. Pour in just enough water to cover them and let it simmer for 30 minutes to 1 hour, or longer if you can.

This will give you a nice pot of stock which you can freeze to use the next time you make a shepherd's pie, or use in an autumn root vegetable risotto — try the Parsnip Risotto on page 194.

North African spiced shank stew
with traveller's couscous

Lamb shanks are delicious. They usually come on the bone and have the sort of meat that just falls apart after a bit of slow-cooking.

SERVES 4

75g (10–12) dried apricots

olive oil

1 lamb shank, bone in

2 onions, thinly sliced

1 tablespoon fresh ginger, peeled and grated

1 teaspoon ground cinnamon

1 teaspoon ground coriander

a generous pinch of saffron

sea salt and black pepper

400g tin tomatoes

400g tin chickpeas, drained and rinsed

1 tablespoon honey

a small handful of freshly chopped coriander to serve

FOR THE TRAVELLER'S COUSCOUS

200g couscous

juice and zest of 1 lemon

1 teaspoon honey

2 tablespoons olive oil

1 garlic clove, finely minced

sea salt and black pepper

350ml boiling hot water, chicken or veg stock

2 tablespoons olives, stoned and finely chopped

50g pine nuts, toasted

1 courgette, coarsely grated

a big handful of fresh mint and/or basil, finely chopped

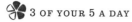 3 OF YOUR 5 A DAY

Soak the apricots in 500ml warm water while you prepare the rest of the stew.

Heat a splash of olive oil in a large flameproof casserole and brown the lamb all over. Set aside.

Fry the onions in the remaining fat until soft (about 5 minutes), then add the ginger, cinnamon, coriander and saffron. Fry until fragrant and well incorporated.

Stir the tomatoes through. Return the lamb to the pan. Tip the water from the soaked apricots over the lamb. Keep the apricots where they are and top back up with warm water.

Bring the stew to the boil. Season with salt and pepper, cover and simmer for 1 hour 30 minutes.

After an hour, add the chickpeas, soaked apricots and honey and continue to simmer gently for an hour until the meat is so tender it falls off the bone. Reserve the remaining apricot-soaking water and use it to top up the stew if it starts getting dry.

To make the Traveller's Couscous, mix the couscous, lemon juice and zest, honey, olive oil and garlic in a bowl or pan you can cover with a lid (or plate). Season with a pinch of salt and a good grinding of black pepper.

Pour in the hot water or stock and cover immediately. Let the water absorb for 10 minutes, then fluff with a fork. Fold in the remaining ingredients.

Serve the stew with fresh coriander over the top and the Traveller's Couscous.

Butternut squash stuffed with lamb, pine nuts and dates

This stuffing is like a Moroccan-spice meatball. The sweetness from the dates and the kick of chilli and spice marry it beautifully to the butternut. Setting it in the squash means you get generous portions of veg wrapped into the package.

SERVES 4

200g minced lamb

1 small onion or a shallot

2 garlic cloves, finely chopped

3 dates, finely chopped

2 tablespoons pine nuts, toasted

½ teaspoon ground cinnamon

a touch of red chilli, deseeded and finely chopped (to taste)

a handful of parsley, mint and/ or coriander

olive oil

1 large or 2 small butternut squash, halved lenghtwise and deseeded

sea salt

balsamic vinegar, to serve

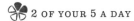 2 OF YOUR 5 A DAY

Mix the lamb, onion, garlic, dates, pine nuts, spice and herbs. Add a pinch of salt. Place the squash on a baking dish and use the mixture to fill the cavities. Splash a bit of olive oil beneath and on top of the squash. Sprinkle a bit of salt over and bake for 1 hour, or until tender. Cover with a baking tray or foil half way through cooking, to prevent the stuffing from burning.

Once cooked, transfer the stuffed squash to plates. If you used one large squash, halve each piece lengthwise to make four portions. Splash a bit of balsamic vinegar over (use aged balsamic if you can). Serve with Traveller's Couscous (see opposite) or a simple salad.

Barbecue

As the dishes in this book call for less meat than you'd normally use, you may find yourself with leftover scraps of meat. Wrap them up, make sure you label them, and pop them in the freezer. When you have a good collection of scraps, defrost them and road test some of the rubs and marinades below. String plenty of veg (and fruits) to your skewers and serve with a big salad and potatoes.

Things to skewer

BEEF Any cut will do. Marinate stewing cuts for longer.

LAMB As above.

PORK Select leaner cuts of pork as too much fat will make your fire hiss. Though, if you're cooking your skewers in the oven, a fattier cut such as pork chops, shoulder or even bacon or belly, will work nicely. Sausages are also delicious on the barbecue.

GAME Cooks beautifully, and quickly, on the grill or in the oven on skewers. Try rabbit, venison, wood pigeon, grouse, you name it.

CHICKEN Any cut will do. A great meat for soaking up marinades.

FISH Any fish will do. Don't forget about shellfish: scallops, prawns, langoustines...

CHEESE Halloumi is ideal for an outdoor barbecue, while cheddar and brie work well on a roasting tray.

BREAD Nuggets of stale bread add variety.

POTATOES Boiled until tender, they're delicious with a bit of crisping up on a skewer.

RICE Cook up a batch of Asian sticky rice, add toasted sesame seeds if you like, then scoop it into balls and it's ready to skewer.

VEGETABLES Cherry tomatoes, whole or sliced mushrooms, courgettes in rounds or ribbons, marinated aubergines, sweet potato cubes...there's a list of ideas paired with each marinade overleaf.

FLAVOURFUL SKEWERS
- branches of bay
- stalks of woody rosemary and thyme
- lemon grass
- bamboo

Marinades and rubs

These marinades and rubs take seconds to mix up. They really can transform odds and ends of vegetables and meat into something rather special. Sometimes I even use them on vegetables, especially when I have a fridge full of odds and ends that need using up.

The method is the same for all of the marinades: mix all the ingredients together, rub into the meat, fish or vegetables of your choice and marinate for at least 30 minutes or up to 48 hours.

Coffee rub

Enough for 200g meat — delicious with beef and venison
Goes well with: mushrooms, sweet potatoes, cooked chestnuts, figs, cooked beetroot and other root veg,

1 tablespoon freshly ground coffee (you can use coffee grounds — a great way of recycling them!)

2 teaspoons brown sugar

2 teaspoons freshly ground black pepper

½ teaspoon dried oregano

½ teaspoon fine sea salt

Smoky rosemary rub

Enough for 200g meat — gorgeous with beef, lamb and fish
Goes well with: tomatoes, aubergines, peppers and courgettes

1½ teaspoons sea salt

1 teaspoon brown sugar

½ teaspoon black pepper, ground

2 tablespoons fresh rosemary, finely chopped

2 garlic cloves, finely minced

2 teaspoons smoky paprika

a pinch of chilli powder, to taste

Guinness mustard

Enough for 200g meat – delicious with rabbit, pork and chicken
Goes well with: cauliflower, new potatoes, asparagus, broccoli

3 tablespoons grainy mustard

1 tablespoon Guinness

1 teaspoon brown sugar

Caribbean-spiced pineapple marinade

Enough for 200g meat — perfect for fish, pork and chicken
Goes well with: balls of sticky rice, slices of runner beans, radishes, fennel, red onions

3 tablespoons fresh pineapple, finely grated (pineapple juice will do)

1½ teaspoons fresh ginger, finely grated

1 tablespoon lime juice

1 teaspoons brown sugar

7 allspice berries, finely ground (about ½ teaspoon)

Curry lime

Enough for 200g meat — perfect for fish, pork, chicken and beef
Goes well with: mango, cucumber, melon and sugar snap peas

2 tablespoons mild curry powder

1 tablespoon lime juice

a grating of lime zest

1 teaspoon honey

Other great rubs and marinades are tucked into other chapters • Tandoori Rub PAGE 144 • 5-Minute BBQ Sauce PAGE 106

PORK

Rare breeds to seek include: Berkshire, Tamworth, Middle White and Gloucester Old Spot, but look out for the many others, too.

One of the lovely things about eating less meat is that I've found I spend more time sourcing it. Seeking meat from rare and unusual breeds has been part of the adventure. It's especially relevant when it comes to pork.

As farming became industrialised after the Second World War, there was a greater emphasis on quantity rather than quality. This resulted in a decline in traditional breeds that thrive outdoors, now classified as rare or heritage breeds. It's vital to support farmers who breed them. These old-fashioned pigs represent a unique piece of the earth's bio-diversity and losing them impoverishes agriculture.

During the last century, 26 native breeds of livestock became extinct in Britain. In the United States, most pork now comes from just four breeds – Yorkshire, Landrace, Hampshire and Duroc. These breeds have been chosen because they can be reared quickly and intensively.

Rare-breeds by contrast are slow-growing and they thrive in natural conditions. You can't intensively farm them – they won't have it. They like to be outside foraging for food, imbibing minerals and nutrients from the soil and breathing fresh air. All of their inherent traits translate to nutritious meat that tastes truly wonderful.

These old-fashioned pigs also have a good layering of fat on the top and are marbled throughout. This is a good thing. In Jennifer McLagan's book *Fat: An Appreciation of a Misunderstood Ingredient*, she makes a convincing argument, which is backed up by medical studies, that fat from grass-fed animals such as heritage pigs has a lot of healthy attributes.

Fat, she argues, 'gives us energy. It boosts the immune system. Some fats have antimicrobial properties. There are vitamins that are only fat-soluble, and fat helps you digest protein.'

Okinawa in Japan has the world's highest life expectancy and the highest percentage of centenarians, and pork lard is their primary cooking fat. If you think about it, animal fats are also the least processed. You're in charge of rendering it out, through cooking, and that's it. The fat from a lovingly-reared animal can be very pure.

So, next time you go out to buy pork, seek a rosy piece of meat that has a layering of fat. It's a healthy sign. It tells you that the animal was raised slowly and for longer. The fat you eat from it has benefits and it lends the meat the most extraordinary flavour.

As American chef Tony Bettencourt says, 'The fat has to come from somewhere. You can drown tasteless pork in cream sauce, disguise it with barbecue sauce or stuff it with cheese to give it some fat and some flavour. Or you can go back to the real thing.'

Other things to consider when sourcing pork are water and nitrites. Water is sometimes added to processed pork products such as ham and bacon to make them heavier, so that they can be sold for more.

Nitrites are the other thing to try to avoid. To cure pork, salt is added. Once the salt works its curing magic, a preserving chemical called nitrite develops naturally. These days, however, nitrites tend to be added to the meat in the beginning of the curing process. This speeds things up and gives the meat an artificial pink tinge. Nitrites offer additional protection against the growth of bacteria, but if the pork is cured with care, in a safe, clean environment, the risks are minimal, making nitrites unnecessary. A number of studies show that this additive can increase the risk of various cancers, so my bid is to avoid them. A growing number of producers now offer nitrite-free options.

Because we seek pork with virtually no fat, pigs are slaughtered younger.

We have a habit of thinking that cheap food equals value, but most often cheap means we're being cheated.

1 PORK LOIN, 5 MEALS

THE MAIN EVENT

Roast pork loin with fennel
and rosemary crackling
PAGE 72

Stuffed apples
PAGE 72

Cider gravy
PAGE 72

Honey mustard parsnips
PAGE 119

Caramelised fennel steaks
PAGE 119

Pudding suggestion:
Dark raspberry truffles
PAGE 210

REMAINS

*Meals to get you through the
week*

Pineapple and ginger rice
with pork
PAGE 78

Quick pork cider stew
with rosemary croutons
PAGE 75
or
Pork and apricot burgers
PAGE 43

Pork and vegetable dumplings
PAGE 76–77

Mexican fried pork wraps
PAGE 73

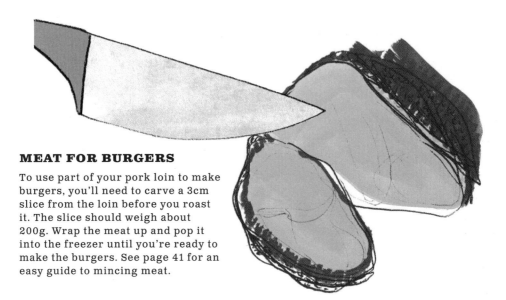

MEAT FOR BURGERS

To use part of your pork loin to make
burgers, you'll need to carve a 3cm
slice from the loin before you roast
it. The slice should weigh about
200g. Wrap the meat up and pop it
into the freezer until you're ready to
make the burgers. See page 41 for an
easy guide to mincing meat.

FIRST QUARTER
If you want to make the **Pork and Apricot Burgers**, use the first part of your pork loin as illustrated left. Alternatively, roast the full joint and use the first few slices from the cooked meat, which are slightly drier. Use them in **Quick Pork Cider Stew**, along with any leftover gravy.

SECOND QUARTER
You'll find the most succulent meat as you move towards the centre of the pork loin. This is a great place to carve a few slices off for your roast dinner.

CRACKLING
Strip off all the crispy crackling from the entire loin to serve with your roast dinner. It's a great treat and makes eating less meat pretty much unnoticeable as the crispy fat has so much flavour.

FAT
You'll probably still have a layer of soft fat beneath the crackling and marbled throughout the joint. Reserve this fat to crisp up for the **Mexican Fried Pork Wraps**.

THIRD QUARTER
Use the meat from the third quarter to fill the **Mexican Fried Pork Wraps**.

FOURTH QUARTER
You don't need very much meat to make the **Pineapple and Ginger Rice** or the **Pork and Vegetable Dumplings**. So, you can quite easily make the last quarter of your pork loin stretch to make these two delicious dishes.

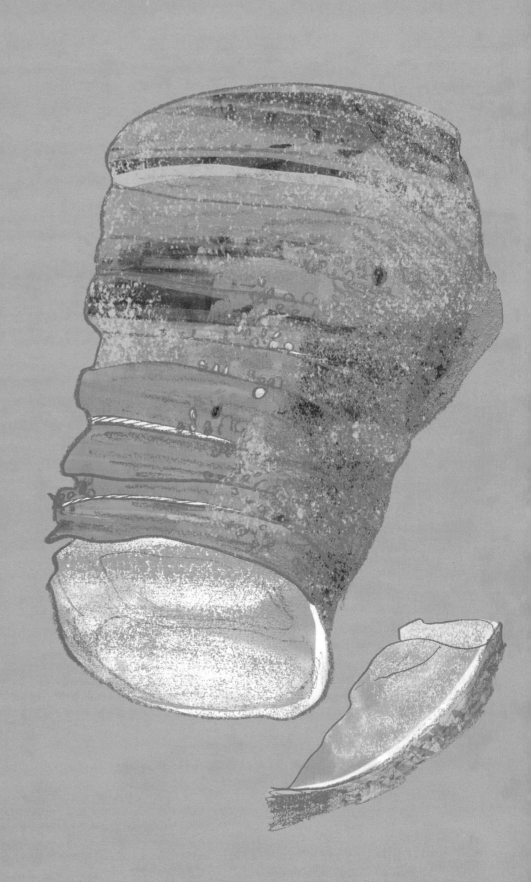

Roast pork loin
with fennel and rosemary crackling, stuffed apples and cider gravy

One of the little treats of this roast menu are the stuffed apples, which you cook alongside the meat and feed with dripping from the pork throughout cooking. This turns the apple stuffing into a sausage-like filling. Serve with Caramelised Fennel Steaks and Honey Mustard Parsnips (see page 119).

SERVES 4

1kg pork loin joint

2 teaspoons sea salt

1 tablespoon rosemary leaves, roughly chopped

¼ teaspoon fennel seeds

FOR THE APPLES

4 apples, cored

75g breadcrumbs

2 tablespoons roasted hazelnuts, finely ground

1 teaspoon rosemary, thyme or sage leaves, roughly chopped

1 garlic clove, roughly chopped

1 teaspoon runny honey

3 tablespoons cider, apple juice or brandy

3–5 tablespoons pan juices

FOR THE GRAVY

1 teaspoon plain flour

375ml cider or apple juice

Preheat the oven to 150°C/gas mark 2.

Pop the pork into a roasting tray. If the skin and fat on top is not scored already, make deep slashes in the fat at 1–2cm intervals, right across the fat and down to the meat. Pat the meat and fat dry.

Mix the salt, rosemary and fennel seeds and; pound them with a pestle and mortar or crush in a bowl. Massage the mixture into the joint, getting as much into the top layer of fat, and right down into the grooves, as possible. Place in the oven for 45 minutes.

While the pork cooks, core the apples. Mix the breadcrumbs with the hazelnuts, herbs and garlic in a food-processor until finely chopped. Add the honey and cider and pulse until combined.

When the pork has cooked for 45 minutes, remove from the oven and crank the heat up to 220°C/gas mark 7.

Spoon 3 tablespoons of the pan juices into the breadcrumbs for the stuffed apples and pulse, adding more juices, if needed, until the mix just starts to come together.

Place the apples in the pan next to the pork. Spoon the mixture into the the apples, packing it in, but not too tightly. Ladle a few more spoonfuls of pan juices over the apples and pop them into the oven, along with the pork for 20–25 minutes, until the crackling is golden and crisp.

Transfer the pork to a plate or platter and leave to rest. Meanwhile, baste the apples with the pan juices and return the apples to the oven. Reduce the temperature to 150°C/gas mark 2. Continue cooking the apples until tender, 15–20 minutes, basting them from time to time.

Remove the apples and set in a serving dish. Place the roasting tin on the top of the stove, over a medium flame, to make the gravy. Sprinkle in the flour and use a wooden spoon to mix it into the pan juices and scrape up all the fat. Slowly stir in the cider and let it bubble up and reduce by half. Strain into a gravy jug and serve.

Mexican fried pork wraps

This is a congenial, help-yourself sort of meal. I often just lay a tray or cutting board full of freshly chopped vegetables and dips so that people can fill their own tortillas. Let the meat feature as simply a garnish on the top – I find that serving the pork on top of all the other ingredients lets it shine through more (in appearance and taste). Also, if you don't have the exact selection of fruits and vegetables I've listed below, you can make up your own selection inspired by the season or what you have in your fridge.

SERVES 4

2 ripe avocados, sliced

4 spring onions, thinly sliced

4 radishes, shaved into slivers

½ cucumber, diced

½ fennel bulb, shaved into fine slivers

1 ripe mango or papaya, diced

2 handfuls cherry tomatoes, quartered

1 lime, quartered

a good handful of fresh coriander and/or mint

50g grated cheese (Cheddar or a semi-hard sheep's milk cheese)

about 2 tablespoons pork fat plucked from your roasting joint, finely chopped

150g leftover roast pork, chopped

1 garlic clove, finely chopped

½ teaspoon ground cumin

½ teaspoon ground coriander

½–1 red chilli, deseeded and finely chopped

8 flour tortilla wraps

 2.5 OF YOUR 5 A DAY

Arrange the avocado, spring onions, radishes, cucumber, fennel, mango or papaya, and cherry tomatoes in little dishes on a cutting board. Add a few lime wedges and herbs, which you can chop or just place in a cup or a jar like a bouquet of flowers. Place the grated cheese in a bowl among the other ingredients.

Melt the fat in a large frying pan (that way you can use the same pan to warm your tortillas – they'll mop up some of those flavours) over a high heat and let it get nice and crispy. Add the pork, garlic, spices and chilli. Fry for 3–5 minutes, just to warm it through. Pinch a few leaves from your herb bouquet to throw on top. Tip the meat into a serving dish and keep warm.

Flash the tortillas in the hot pan, just warming one side. Pile on to plates and let the filling of the tortillas begin.

Quick pork cider stew with rosemary croûtons

You can whip up an almost instant stew using leftover meat because you've already slowly cooked the meat, developing all its flavour and texture. This dish is also a great way to use up any leftover gravy. If you have a pot of crème fraîche or mascarpone in the fridge, add a bit less meat and stir some through at the end.

SERVES 4

about 1 tablespoon fat trimmed from roast pork, finely chopped

olive oil

2 apples, peeled, cored and cut into slices

8 prunes, roughly chopped

2 onions, sliced

2 carrots, peeled and cut into medium dice

2 parsnips and/or a small fennel bulb, cut into medium dice (peel parsnips if you like)

4 sprigs of rosemary, leaves only, finely chopped

200g leftover pork, shredded or roughly diced

500ml cider, apple juice and/or leftover cider gravy

1 small cinnamon stick, a bay leaf and/or fresh ginger (optional – to suit mood and availability)

2–3 slices of bread, preferably stale, torn or cut into 2cm cubes

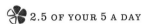 2.5 OF YOUR 5 A DAY

Place a pot or casserole dish over high heat. When hot, add the fat, turn down the heat and let it sizzle and render out for a few minutes. Stir all the fruits and vegetables through the fat and top up with olive oil if needed. Pop a lid on and let them sweat down, on medium-low heat, for about 15 minutes, stirring occasionally.

Take the lid off, turn up the heat then add the rosemary leaves and sizzle until they pick up a bit of colour. Add the meat, then splash in the gravy, if you have any left from your roast. If not, add a bit of the cider or apple juice. You could also add a little splash of brandy for extra richness. Let it sizzle and soak into the veg.

Add the cinnamon, bay leaf or ginger, if using. Top up with the remaining cider or juice, just enough to cover, and let it bubble up at high heat for a few minutes, just until the stew has thickened slightly. If it hasn't, ladle 2 spoonfuls of broth into a tea cup and whisk with 1 teaspoon flour until there are no lumps. Stir this into the stew and it should do the trick. Taste and adjust the seasoning as needed.

When the stew is ready, set aside and quickly fry your torn bread hunks in a bit of olive oil with the garlic and rosemary. Season with salt and scatter them in the stew.

Delicious on its own or paired with mash and a green salad.

NOTE If you want to make this recipe without roasting an entire joint of pork, you could pan-fry a 200g pork chop and use that. Make a gravy by stirring 1 teaspoon flour into the fat from your chop. Set it over medium-high heat and whisk in a bottle of apple cider, little by little, until you have a nice gravy to use as the base of your stew. Trim and chop some of the fat from the pork to sizzle the vegetables in.

Pork and vegetable dumplings

If you love dim sum, you'll adore these homemade dumplings, which are surprisingly easy to make. They're delicious as a main course when served with a side of stir-fried vegetables, bowls of rice and a pot of green tea.

MAKES ABOUT 30 DUMPLINGS, ENOUGH FOR 4–6 PEOPLE AS A MAIN COURSE

1 tablespoon finely grated fresh ginger

1 garlic clove, finely minced

¼ red chilli, deseeded and finely chopped (optional)

1 tablespoon soy sauce

1 tablespoon rice, balsamic or cider vinegar

1 teaspoon honey

150–200g leftover roast pork, chopped to a mince-like texture

olive or sunflower oil, for frying

1 medium carrot, peeled and finely diced

½ sweet red pepper, deseeded and finely diced

8 spring onions, finely chopped

a handful of fresh coriander, finely chopped

a splash of sesame oil (optional)

dumpling wrappers from a Chinese grocer, or make your own (see recipe opposite)

a handful of whole coriander leaves to garnish

❀ 1 OF YOUR 5 A DAY, 2.5 IF SERVED WITH STIR-FRIED VEGETABLES

Mix the ginger, garlic, chilli, soy, vinegar and honey in a medium-sized bowl. Add the pork and fold through.

Place a wok or frying pan over medium heat. Add a splash of oil. Sauté the vegetables until tender. Add the pork and marinade and stir-fry over medium-high heat until the vegetables look quite soft.

Put the mixture into a food-processor — do this in batches, if needed, and pulse to grind until finely minced. This will give you a smoother dumpling filler, as you don't want it to be too lumpy. Tip the mixture back into the frying pan. Add coriander and a splash of sesame oil, if using, and combine.

Place a slightly rounded teaspoon of filling in the centre of a wrapper and moisten the surrounding area with water. Fold in half to form a crescent and press to seal. Repeat with remaining filling and wrappers.

Put some oil in a large frying pan. When the oil is warm, place the dumplings in the pan with sufficient space in between. Allow the skin to crisp and brown, then add a little hot water (2–3 tablespoons) and cover for 5 minutes, so that the steaming effect can cook the dumplings through. Once there is no more water left, transfer the dumplings to a platter. You'll have to do this in batches. Scatter over a few handfuls of fresh coriander leaves to garnish — and eat!

Delicious with soy sauce for dipping and a side of stir-fried vegetables.

For the homemade dumpling wrappers

*This is so easy. In fact, you'll spend less time making these than you would
hunting them down in a shop, unless you happen to live in Chinatown.*

¼ teaspoon sea salt

225ml lukewarm water (100ml
boiling water and 125ml cool
tap water)

½ teaspoon olive or
vegetable oil

250g plain white flour, plus
more for dusting

In a jug, whisk the salt into the warm water until dissolved, then add the
oil. Set aside. Tip the flour into a large bowl and add the water mixture.
Stir until the dough comes together in a large, clumpy ball. Cover and
leave to rest for 15 minutes.

Tip the dough onto a large mound of flour. Roll it through the flour,
kneading it until elastic and shiny. Add more flour or water if needed.

Dust a large cutting board with flour. Pinch a cherry-sized ball of dough,
and roll as thinly as you can. Use a large round cutter (about 8cm in
diameter) to make a circular wrapper. Fill as instructed on the left.
Continue with the remaining dough. Place the filled dumplings on a
well-floured baking sheet until ready to cook.

Pineapple and ginger rice with pork

This is a great one to cook up as you approach the end of your roasted pork joint because there's so much flavour and texture in the dish that you really don't need any meat at all. However, a bit of roast pork folded through it is like the icing on the cake.

SERVES 4

150g brown long grain or brown basmati rice

225ml water

sea salt and black pepper

olive oil or pork fat

2 onions, finely chopped

2 carrots, peeled and finely diced

3cm piece of fresh ginger, peeled and finely chopped or grated

1 pineapple, halved, flesh scooped out and roughly chopped into cubes

200g leftover roast pork, shredded or roughly chopped

100g pea shoots or garden peas

a handful of fresh mint, leaves chopped

a handful of cashew nuts, toasted

a dash of soy sauce

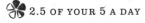 2.5 OF YOUR 5 A DAY

Place the rice in a saucepan and cover with 225ml water. Add a pinch of salt. Pop a lid on and simmer for 25 minutes, or until all the water is absorbed. Keep the lid on and let it sit for 5 minutes. You can make the rice a day in advance. If so, chill straight away.

Place a wok or large frying pan over medium heat. Add a splash of oil or fat. When hot, add the onions, carrots and ginger. Sauté until tender.

Add the rice and fold into the vegetables. Smooth the whole thing into the pan as if you're slathering cake batter into a cake tin. The idea here is to press the rice into the pan and allow it to pick up a bit of colour. Allow to sizzle away for a few minutes. Use a large spoon or spatula to scrape the rice from the bottom of the pan and fold through. Do this a few times until the rice starts to brown just a little.

Add the pineapple and fold through. Let it fry for a few moments. Add the pork and peas. If using garden peas, let them warm through. If using pea shoots, fold them through, along with the mint and cashew nuts, right before serving. Taste. Season with salt, pepper and a dash of soy sauce, if needed.

BLT with avocado

This is the perfect Saturday morning treat after a long week and an even longer Friday night. Instead of mayo, mop up all that amazing bacon grease in the bottom of the pan. Fat from a well-sourced slab of bacon is better for you than a blob of factory-made mayo. Get a boost of vitamin C and an extra portion of fruit and veg by washing it down with a glass of OJ.

FOR EACH BACON SANDWICH, YOU NEED

2 slices bacon, back or streaky

2 slices bread from a good loaf

½ ripe avocado

sea salt and freshly ground black pepper

1 small-medium tomato, thinly sliced

a few crisp lettuce leaves

a few glugs of olive oil

🌸 2 OF YOUR 5 A DAY, 3 WITH 150ML OF JUICE

Grill or fry your bacon until golden. I normally heat the oven grill to the highest setting, warm the grill pan and then lay the bacon when it's so hot it sizzles. I then turn the heat down a bit and grill for 7–10 minutes, until crispy all around the edges.

Scoop the avocado flesh out and slather it over one side of the bread. Sprinkle with a pinch of salt and some pepper.

Lay the cooked bacon over the avocado. Use the other slice of bread to mop up all the bacon fat in the pan. Top the bacon with the tomato slices and some lettuce then sandwich the two pieces of bread together. Bliss, especially if you're eating it in bed...after 11am.

Quick Catalan chorizo stew

Try to seek out a really good, naturally cured chorizo for this dish. One bearing the words '100% pure-bred Ibérico de Bellota' is the best you can get. Ibérico is a rare breed of pig related to wild boar. The 'de Bellota' refers to the fact that the pig has grazed solely on grass and acorns for the last six months of its life. The taste is extraordinary and the fat marbled through it is on par, in health and flavour, with that of a fine olive oil.

SERVES 4

glug of olive oil

2 red peppers

1 large onion, peeled and chopped

2 garlic cloves, finely chopped

150g cooking chorizo, sliced into 2cm hunks (if using cured chorizo, finely chop)

400g tinned chickpeas, drained

2–3 sprigs of rosemary, leaves roughly chopped

800g tinned tomatoes

2 tablespoons raisins or sultanas

a splash of red wine or sherry (optional, but it does add a great deal of richness)

a pinch of paprika

juice and zest of ½ lemon

200g baby leaf spinach

3 tablespoons pine nuts, toasted

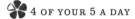 4 OF YOUR 5 A DAY

Preheat the oven to 200°C/gas mark 6. Place the peppers in the oven and roast for 30 minutes, turning once. Leave to cool, remove the skin and seeds and roughly chop.

Splash a glug of olive oil in a large frying pan and fry the onions until soft. Add the peppers and cook for a moment, then add the garlic and chorizo. Fry until the chorizo has warmed through. Add the chickpeas, rosemary, and lemon zest and juice, and coat in the delicious, reddish oil. Stir in the tomatoes and raisins and let it bubble away for a few minutes. Taste and add a splash of wine or sherry, if you fancy, and a pinch of paprika, if needed. Fold the spinach into the stew, and cook for a moment.

Finish with a glug of olive oil, the pine nuts and herbs. Serve with warm crusty bread and a bowl of olives.

Bohemian goulash

In Hungary, goulash is served with pillowy dumplings or butter beans to help soak up all the gorgeous flavours. I've gone for the latter as they add extra protein and an additional vegetable serving. They're also a lot easier than dumplings!

SERVES 6

4 red peppers

250g diced pork

sea salt and black pepper

2 garlic cloves, finely minced

2 onions, thinly sliced

a hunk of fresh red chilli, deseeded and finely chopped (use as little or as much as you like)

2 tablespoons smoky paprika

2 teaspoons caraway seeds, ground

1 ½ teaspoons dried oregano

400g good-quality tinned plum tomatoes

2 tablespoons red wine vinegar

400g tinned butter beans, drained

TO SERVE

50g crème fraîche, sour cream or Greek-style yogurt

1 lemon or lime

a handful of fresh coriander or parsley

basmati rice

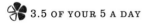 3.5 OF YOUR 5 A DAY

Preheat the oven to 170°C/gas mark 3.

Roast the peppers in a roasting tin until they're soft and just starting to blacken, about 30 minutes. Set aside to cool.

Season the pork generously with salt and pepper and rub in the garlic. Place a large pot over medium-high heat. Add a good glug of olive oil. Add the pork. Cook for about 10 minutes to render out the fat and give it a caramely edge.

While the pork sizzles, slip the skins off the peppers (keep them in the pan to accumulate more juices), pop the stems off and scoop out the seeds and discard. Pull each pepper into 1–2cm-thick ribbons.

When the pork has cooked, remove it from the pot with a slotted spoon, set on a plate and put it to one side.

Gloss the pot with a few more glugs of oil. Add the onions, stir around to mop up any brown bits left from the pork and gently fry for 15 minutes. Fold in the chilli, paprika, caraway seeds and oregano. Add 2 tablespoons water and give it a good stir. Cook for a minute.

Add the peppers and all the juices you collected from them, the pork, the tinned tomatoes and 500ml of water. Give everything a good mix. Add the vinegar. Bring to the boil, put the lid on top, then place in the oven for 3 hours.

Remove the goulash from the oven and stir in the butter beans. Return the pot to the oven while you make the rice. This will give the butter beans a chance to warm through.

Dish out the rice. Spoon the goulash on top. Finish each dish with a squeeze of lemon or lime, a dollop of crème fraîche, sour cream or

Bacon and butterbean soup with buttered bread

The bacon adds so much flavour to this dish that you only need 5–6 rashers to give the vegetable-rich soup real meaty depth. This means there's room in the equation for generous slicks of butter on the accompanying bread.

SERVES 4

olive oil

150g smoky bacon, cut into 1cm pieces

1 onion, finely chopped

3 garlic cloves, finely chopped

1 leek, white and light green part only, thinly sliced

2 carrots, peeled and cut into 2cm dice

2 ribs celery, cut into 1cm dice

2 handfuls of seasonal veg: diced pumpkin, fresh peas, chopped asparagus or diced root veg

800g tinned butter beans, drained

a few sprigs of thyme, leaves only

1 litre chicken or veg stock

a handful of basil leaves, roughly torn

sea salt and black pepper

TO SERVE

fresh herbs

a good loaf of bread

50g nice butter

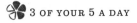 3 OF YOUR 5 A DAY

Heat a glug of olive oil in a large saucepan. When it's hot, add the bacon and onion. Cook over medium heat for 5 minutes until the onion has softened and the bacon is cooked.

Add the garlic, leek, carrots, celery and your pick of seasonal veg. Cover and leave to soften over a low heat for 15 minutes, stirring occasionally.

Add the butter beans, thyme and the stock. Bring to the boil and simmer for 20 minutes until the beans are tender.

Spoon two large ladles of the mixture into a blender and whizz to a smooth purée. Stir this back into the soup so that it thickens a little. Season and serve with a drizzle of olive oil, fresh herbs and thick slabs of buttered bread.

Mini hot dogs with piccalilli salad

Sausages in their own right are a way of stretching meat as they're a mix of ground meat, spices, fat and breadcrumbs. When sourcing them, though, go for the sausages with the highest proportion of meat – 85 per cent meat content is the best.

SERVES 4–6

FOR THE PICCALILLI SALAD

100ml malt or red wine vinegar

100ml water

4 teaspoons golden caster sugar

¼ teaspoon ground allspice

¼ teaspoon ground nutmeg

1 heaped teaspoon fresh ginger, peeled and grated

1 garlic clove, crushed with ½ teaspoon salt

1 medium cauliflower, cut into bite-sized florets

1 onion, finely diced

2 courgettes, quartered lengthwise and then cut into 2–3cm hunks

225g green beans, trimmed and cut into 3cm diagonal slices

1 tablespoon mustard powder

1 heaped teaspoon ground turmeric

1 heaped teaspoon flour

salad leaves or cauliflower greens

FOR THE HOT DOGS

8–12 free-range local mini sausages or chipolatas

1–2 bakery baguettes or individual hot dog buns

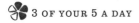 3 OF YOUR 5 A DAY

First, make the piccalilli salad. Place the vinegar, water, sugar, allspice, nutmeg, fresh ginger, garlic and salt in a wide-bottomed pot. Simmer for a moment, gently whisking, until the sugar has dissolved and all the flavours have mixed. Add the vegetables and fold through. Simmer, lid on, for 5–8 minutes, until the veg has softened a tiny bit – you want it to be crisp but also a tad bit soft so it can soak up all the spices.

Drain the veg, reserving the vinegar mix. Ladle 3–4 tablespoons of the vinegar into a small bowl and whisk with the mustard powder, turmeric and flour until you have a fairly smooth paste. Spoon this into the remaining vinegar and whisk over gentle heat until it's smooth and starts to thicken a bit. Allow it to cool and then pour over the veg.

Refrigerate the piccalilli salad for at least 30 minutes or up to a week in advance.

When you are ready to cook the hot dogs, simply cook the sausages to your liking and wrap in the bread. Mix the salad leaves or cauliflower greens through the piccalilli salad at the last minute and serve with the hot dogs.

A hearty sausage minestrone

This is a summery, Mediterranean-style minestrone enriched with nuggets of caramelised sausage. See ideas below for seasonal twists.

SERVES 4–6

500ml chicken or vegetable stock

1 potato, peeled and diced

1 carrot, peeled and diced

1 bay leaf

100g pasta (a small elbow or shell shape is ideal, but you can use any shape, including broken strands of spaghetti)

2 large pork sausages

olive oil

1 small onion, chopped

3–4 garlic cloves, crushed

1 large courgette, diced

400g tin chopped tomatoes

a good glug of balsamic vinegar

a splash of red wine (optional)

400g tin red kidney or cannellini beans, drained

a good handful of fresh basil

50g Parmesan cheese, grated

sea salt and black pepper

2.5 TO 3 PORTIONS OF YOUR 5 A DAY

Warm the stock. Add the potato, carrot and bay leaf. Cook over medium-low heat for about 15 minutes. Then add the pasta and cook for 10–15 minutes, or until the pasta is al dente and the potatoes tender.

Snip or slice the sausages into 2cm pieces, removing the skins. Warm a splash of olive oil in a good-sized saucepan or pot. Fry the sausage until golden. Add the onion and garlic and cook until soft. Add the courgette and sauté over medium-high heat until it starts to pick up a bit of colour.

Pour in the tinned tomatoes and a good splash of balsamic or wine, if using; let it bubble up for a minute. Reduce the heat then add the beans, potatoes, carrots, pasta and any remaining stock. Let it bubble up. Simmer for 10 minutes to let the flavours mingle. Turn off the heat. Divide between bowls, adding a glug of olive oil, a handful of basil, a heap of Parmesan and freshly ground pepper over the top of each.

Delicious with Pan-fried Rosemary Bread (page 99) and avocado slices.

SEASONAL VARATIONS

SPRING: use new potatoes and bunched carrots in the early part of the recipe. Opt for sprouting broccoli instead of courgettes. Finish with a good heap of wild garlic and spring herbs.

AUTUMN: opt for pumpkin or squash in place of courgettes.

WINTER: swap courgettes for root vegetables or diced winter celery. Add kale and rosemary instead of basil.

POULTRY

Chickens offer wholesome, nourishing meat. They make soup that's good for the soul – Jewish penicillin to help fight colds. Chicken and other poultry have an amazing ability to absorb flavours, becoming almost sponge-like in their ability to mop up sauces. Poultry is easy to cook and is just wonderful in so many ways.

It's easy to understand our desire for it, but over the years we've gone a bit too mad for poultry – chicken, in particular. I was shocked when I uncovered figures illustrating exactly how much chicken and other poultry we now consume, especially when compared to what our grandparents ate. Herbert Hoover famously promised 'a chicken in every pot'. It was well-meaning and noble then, but in the 21st century Americans eat 450 per cent more poultry than their forefathers did in 1910.

In Britain, the number of chickens reared for the table rocketed from 1 million in 1950 to 860 million in 2007. If all these chickens were reared naturally – clucking around outdoors, pecking at the grass and eating bugs and worms – this wouldn't be an issue.

More than 99 per cent of chicken sold in America is factory farmed. In Britain, only 5 per cent of chickens are reared outdoors.

However, to cater to such gross demand, shortcuts are taken. Chickens are bred to grow faster and faster, making them crippled under their own unnatural weights. Most of the chickens we eat today live in artificially lit warehouses. Their life span keeps getting shorter and shorter. On the whole, their diet is man-made and consists of soy beans that were grown on cleared rainforest, and many are often genetically modified to increase yields. In the year leading up to August 2004, an area of rainforest the size of Belgium was cut down to provide land for crops such as soya which is exported to feed livestock in America and Europe.

Seek outdoor-reared, grass-fed poultry. It's so much better for you.

This seems completely mad. I think that most people just don't know about it. I'm hoping that if you didn't, but now you do, that you will try to buy poultry from animals that are reared outdoors and fed on grass. There are so many benefits in doing so – most of them are related to your health.

Chickens reared outdoors and allowed to run around and eat omega-rich grass are happy little things. They live longer, healthier lives and these things are reflected in their meat. It has 21 per cent less total fat, 30 per cent less saturated fat, and 28 per cent fewer calories than chickens reared indoors. It also offers 50 per cent more vitamin A and 100 per cent more omega-3 fatty acids, of which our diets are severely deficient.

Demanding properly grown food could spark a revolution.

You will have to pay extra to get a good bird (do you really want to give your money to those who rear poultry intensively?) but you get a better deal. So does the chicken, and no rainforests need to be cut down either. My plea to you is to buy a better bird (outdoor and grass-fed are key). Make the most of it, and enjoy every morsel. You will, as a good healthy bird tastes marvellous.

1 CHICKEN, 5 MEALS

GIBLETS

The liver is the silky, smooth burgundy bit in the giblet pack. It makes the most delicious pâté. Other giblet bits include the neck, heart, kidneys and sometimes the gizzard. Don't be squeamish, these bits are loaded with essential nutrients (ones we need more of) and they make a wonderful sauce for pasta.

BREASTS
For your roast dinner, carve from the two breasts. 50g is about the size of half a breast. (If you or some of your diners prefer dark meat, pull meat from one of the legs.)

FIRST LEG
Use the meat from one of the legs to make the **Mango Chicken Salad.** (Swap with breast meat if you served some of this meat for your roast dinner.)

SECOND LEG
Shred this meat for use in the **Italian Chicken Soup.** The leftover meat can be stored in the fridge for up to 4 days.

WINGS AND CARCASS
You can get a surprising amount of meat from the wings and the rest of the carcass. Check along the backbone and collar. You can also use this meat in the salad or soup.

BONES AND SKIN
Use the roasted bones and the skin as the base for your stock. All you need are some basic vegetables such as onions, carrots and celery and a few peppercorns to make a good stock. This will form the base for the **Italian Chicken Soup.** Make the stock the day of your roast dinner, or you can refrigerate the bones for up to 2 days before making.

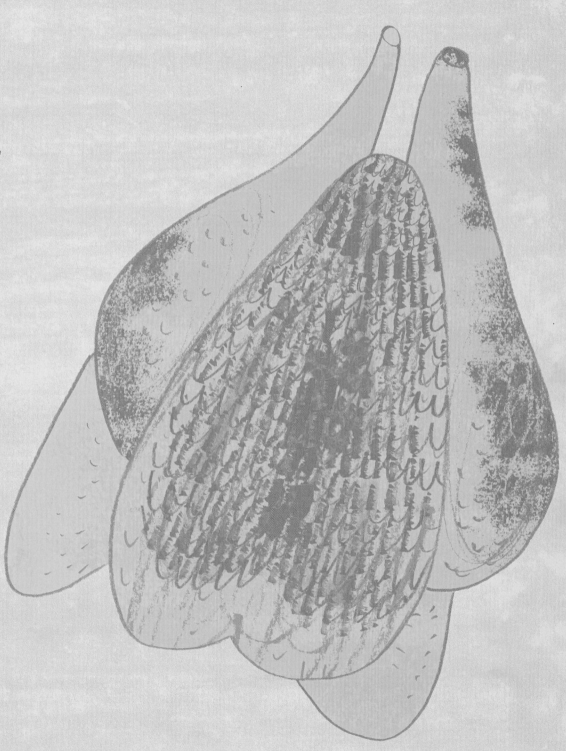

Effortless roast chicken

Get your hands on a good chicken – one that's been pecking at the grass and running around the field for a good period – to make the most delicious roast chicken with absolutely no effort. You don't even need a sliver of butter to make it taste good.

Here, I've laid the bird on a bed of butternut squash to help soak up all the buttery, butter-free juices. Heavenly! Serve with two seasonal sides (see pages 116–120 for ideas.)

SERVES 4

1.4kg chicken

1 butternut squash, peeled and sliced wedges

3 garlic cloves, unpeeled

2 teaspoons sea salt

a few sprigs of thyme, leaves only

Preheat the oven to 230°C/gas mark 8.

Scatter the butternut squash wedges and garlic in the roasting tray.

Remove the giblets from the chicken (I once forgot to do this!). To keep the breasts extra tender, use a bit of string to tie the ends of the legs to where they're crisscrossing over the breasts, pointing up toward the ceiling. Pat the chicken dry all over (this helps crisp up the skin). Set the chicken on top of the squash and sprinkle salt generously over it.

Place the chicken in the oven, ensuring that the temperature has reached full whack.

Cook for 1 hour — no peeking as this will let all the heat out and prevent your bird from cooking through. When the timer goes off, turn the oven off but keep your bird in for 15 minutes longer.

Remove the chicken from the oven and place on a platter. Transfer your squash to a serving dish, sprinkle thyme leaves on top and pop in the oven to keep them warm.

Make your gravy and sides while the chicken rests.

How to make gravy

juices from the roasting tin

LIQUID OPTIONS
(YOU WILL NEED 250ML TOTAL)

wine Red, white, pink or
fortified — i.e. port or a
dessert wine

juice Apple, orange or
elderflower

stock Veg or chicken

spirit Calvados, a peaty whisky
or brandy, plus stock – if going
down this route, add 50ml
spirit to 200ml stock

Place the roasting tin on the hob directly over a low flame. If there's
quite a bit of liquid, let it reduce down to about 4 tablespoons.

Slowly add some liquid – choose from the list on the left.

Let everything bubble up and reduce by half until it reaches the desired
consistency. Taste. Add extra flavouring if you like – see the box below.
Taste again and once you're happy, serve.

EXTRA FLAVOURING

Spice (saffron or cinnamon)

Herbs (tarragon or thyme)

Fruit (ripe blackberries,
cherries or apple slices)

Veg (caramelised onions or
wild mushrooms)

A pinch of sugar, drop of honey
or balsamic vinegar

Salt and pepper

How to make stock

chicken bones and skin

2–3 carrots, chopped

2 onions, chopped

2–3 garlic cloves, crushed

a handful of parsley or thyme

peppercorns

Toss the chicken bones and skin into a pot. Top with the carrot, onion,
garlic and parsley or thyme.

Pour enough water to cover and simmer for 1 hour. Drain, cool and store
in plastic pots in the fridge (up to 2 days) or the freezer (6 months).

STORAGE TIPS AND USES FOR STOCK

Keep a bag of veg and herb scraps - such as dark green leek ends,
the woody ends of asparagus, fennel tops, stripped sprigs of thyme in
the fridge. These can be added to the stockpot.

The stock above will give you a few portions for the freezer. You
can melt the stock from frozen and use it immediately. To loosen
frozen stock from a plastic pot, just run the pot under warm water
until the frozen block of stock loosens and slips out. Place in a
saucepan over medium heat to melt. This stock makes a great base
for risottos and soups.

Jar of country pâté

Silky burgundy chicken livers are like nuggets of gold, especially when whipped with butter and brandy. This creates a pâté you'd swoon over in a restaurant. Why shouldn't you have it at home?

Pair it with a glass of wine and some celery, radish and figs and have it as a light meal in the evening. It also makes a great at-desk lunch. In some countries, nearly a third of a chicken is wasted, so this is a great way to make more of your bird. Think of it as a free meal.

SERVES 2–6

1 chicken liver

a lump of butter the size
of the liver (25–50g), plus
2 tablespoons to seal the top

1–2 prunes, thinly sliced

1 teaspoonful thyme leaves

1 tiny garlic clove, crushed

3 tablespoons brandy

sea salt and pepper

WITH CRUDITÉS, YOU CAN
RACK UP 2.5 OF YOUR 5 A DAY

Place a small frying pan over medium heat. Add a nugget of the butter – about half a tablespoon. When it's frothy, add the liver. Cook for a minute or two on each side, just until it goes from burgundy to a pinky grey. Put the liver in a food-processor or blender.

Place the frying pan back on the heat. Add the prunes, thyme and garlic. Let them soften for a moment. Carefully add the brandy. Let it bubble up and reduce just a tad. Scrape into the food-processor with the liver. Add the remaining butter (bar what you're reserving for the top) and blitz until creamy. Spoon into a small jam or Kilner jar.

Give the pan you've been using a quick wash. Gently melt the remaining butter in it; don't let it froth up. Pour into the jar, over the pâté, giving it a nice, buttery seal. Eat within 3–4 days.

SERVING SUGGESTIONS: Cucumber • Celery • Radishes • Pears • Apples • Grapes • Figs • Plums or prunes • Rustic Oatcakes (see page 188) • A glass of wine

VARIATION

You can also make this recipe with duck or goose livers, which are quite a bit larger than chicken livers. Most duck livers I've used are around 100g. Weigh the liver and measure an equal amount of butter, or just cut a piece of butter that looks roughly the same size.

Tagliatelle
with creamy white wine, giblet and mushroom sauce

Ok, giblets aren't very attractive but they are extremely rich in nutrients such as selenium and Coenzyme Q10, which are hard to get elsewhere. This lovely dish is inspired by a woman (thank you, Ann) I met on a cookery course. Give it a go, you'll be pleasantly surprised.

SERVES 4

giblets from 1 chicken

1 tablespoon thyme leaves

3 garlic cloves, finely chopped

juice and zest of 1 lemon

300g tagliatelle, or any pasta shape you like

1 head of broccoli, cut into small florets with a bit of wispy stalk at the ends

olive oil

1 small onion or banana shallot, finely chopped

300g mushrooms (wild ones work really nicely but chestnut or portobellos will do)

300ml white wine (a sweeter wine like Riesling works well here)

150ml double cream

a handful parsley or tarragon, leaves chopped

sea salt and black pepper

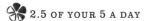 2.5 OF YOUR 5 A DAY

Get a pot of boiling water on the go for your pasta. Add the neck from the giblets to the water with a pinch of salt.

Let it bubble away for a few minutes while you chop the giblets. You can use all the remaining giblets for the sauce, or you can save the liver for the pâté on page 94. Use a sharp knife or kitchen scissors to cut the everything into 1cm (or smaller) pieces. Set aside. Mix the giblets with the thyme, garlic and lemon zest.

Add the pasta to the pan and cook until al dente. Add the broccoli and cook for a minute longer. Drain. Remove the neck – you can shred a bit of the meat off, if you like, and add to the pasta. Season and drizzle a bit of olive oil over. Set in a warm spot.

The sauce only takes a few minutes to make. Place a large pan over medium heat. Add a splash of olive oil. Once hot, add the onion or shallot and the mushrooms. Sauté until golden, add more olive oil if needed.

Add the garlic, giblets, thyme leaves, lemon juice and zest. Cook for a few minutes, until the giblets turn a mushroomy browny-grey. Splash in the wine. Let it bubble up and reduce a bit. Lower the heat. Stir in the cream. Season.

Reheat the pasta and broccoli for a minute, if needed. Pile onto plates and pour the sauce over the top. Finish with a dusting of herbs. Delicious with a glass of wine and some bread to mop up the sauce.

Mango chicken salad

This is a family favourite – we have it every time we roast a chicken. It's great because you don't need loads of meat to make it work. I like to use the meat from one of the chicken legs. The dark meat adds heaps of flavour, while the white meat soaks up all the sweet mango juices. It takes minutes to make and is a salad even children seem to love.

SERVES 4

2 ripe mangoes, cut into 2–3cm hunks

3 ripe avocados, cut into 2–3cm hunks

200g leftover roast chicken, shredded

sea salt and black pepper

juice of 1 lemon or 2 limes

4 large handfuls of watercress, rocket and/or baby leaf spinach

olive oil

1 handful of basil or other soft green herbs, leaves torn

50g pine nuts, toasted

3 OF YOUR 5 A DAY

Mix the mango, avocado and chicken in a bowl. Season well. Squeeze the juice from the lemon or limes over the top. Give it a good mix.

Pile onto plates with the leaves. Drizzle a bit of olive oil over the top. Scatter herbs and pine nuts over the top. Serve.

STORING LEFTOVER CHICKEN

Cooked chicken will keep on the bone (if the bird is wrapped up and stored in the fridge) for 2 days. Meat off the bone will keep for up to 4 days, which is ideal for the 'Remains' recipes. When cooking with leftover meat it is important to ensure the meat is heated through fully.
  You can also freeze the meat (off the bone), provided you defrost it thoroughly, use within 24 hours and reheat it all the way through. This meat is ideal for soups, stews and pies.

Italian chicken soup

A hearty chicken stock makes this dish, so put the bones and leftover skin from your roast chicken to work. The stock will lend so much richness and body that you really only need very little meat. This is my favourite version of chicken noodle soup.

SERVES 4 GENEROUSLY

olive oil

1 onion, chopped

2 carrots, diced

½ large or 1 small fennel bulb, diced

3 ribs celery, diced

2 medium courgettes, diced

3 large garlic cloves, chopped

1 teaspoon fennel seeds

1 litre chicken stock

100g small pasta or broken spaghetti

150g diced cooked chicken

1 red chilli, deseeded and chopped, or a pinch of dried chilli flakes (optional)

a handful of fresh basil leaves, roughly torn

a small nugget of Parmesan cheese

 2.5 OF YOUR 5 A DAY

Heat a splash of oil in a large saucepan or pot. Gently sauté the vegetables, garlic and fennel seeds until nicely softened, about 20 minutes.

Meanwhile, bring the stock to the boil. Add the pasta and cook it until al dente.

Stir the chicken in with the pasta to warm it though. Pour the stock, chicken and pasta in with the vegetables once the veg are cooked.

If everyone eating the soup likes a chilli kick, add it now. Otherwise, ladle the soup into bowls and top with chilli, basil and Parmesan.

Lovely served with Pan-Fried Rosemary Bread (see below).

PAN-FRIED ROSEMARY BREAD

Splash a bit of olive oil into a warm pan. Add a sprig or two of rosemary, a large crushed garlic and a pinch of sea salt. Press thick slices of good bread into the hot, fragrant oil and cook on each (or just one) side until golden.

Chicken paillard with lentils, caper salsa and a taste of the season

A chicken breast can easily serve two people. The joy of this dish is that the flattened breasts also cook a lot faster.

SERVES 4

2 skinless chicken breasts

sea salt and black pepper

4 tablespoons plain flour, seasoned

olive oil

FOR THE MUSTARDY PUY LENTILS

olive oil

1 large onion, finely chopped

3 garlic cloves, chopped

200g puy lentils

1 bay leaf

400ml chicken stock or water

1–2 tablespoons Dijon mustard

a good splash of balsamic vinegar

sea salt and black pepper

FOR THE MINTY OLIVE CAPER SALSA

2 tablespoons capers

a large handful of Kalamata olives, destoned and roughly chopped

a handful of fresh mint leaves, roughly chopped

a squeeze of lemon

✿ 3 OF YOUR 5 A DAY SERVED WITH A MOUND OF LENTILS AND TWO HANDFULS OF SEASONAL VEG

First make the Mustardy Puy Lentils. Add a splash of olive oil to a pot. Sauté the onion and garlic over medium-low heat for 15 minutes, until soft and starting to caramelise.

Fold the lentils and bay leaf through. Pour over the stock. Pop a lid on and cook for 40 minutes, or until the lentils are tender.

Once the lentils are cooked, season well. Stir through the mustard little by little until you've got the perfect hit of mustard for your taste buds. Add a splash of balsamic vinegar for a touch of sweetness.

Cut each chicken breast in half horizontally. Season well. Place on a cutting board (one you normally use for meat) or between sheets of clingfilm and flatten with a meat mallet or rolling pin.

Lightly dust each piece of chicken with flour.

Heat the oil in a non-stick frying pan and sear the chicken in batches over medium heat for 2–4 minutes on each side until cooked through.

For the Minty Olive Caper Salsa, mix all the ingredients in a small bowl.

Serve the chicken with the lentils, salsa and a Taste of the Season (see below).

A TASTE OF THE SEASON

SPRING: asparagus and bunched carrots with a handful of herbs
SUMMER: green beans and a colourful selection of summer tomatoes
AUTUMN: pan-fried slices of squash and sautéed baby spinach leaves
WINTER: a salad made with watercress, orange or clementine segments and the seeds and juice from a pomegranate

Sweet and sour chicken

It's so easy to make your own version of this Chinese take-away classic. The joy of making your own means you know where the meat has come from. It's also a great dish for packing in the veg. Feel free to swap any of the veggies I've listed below with ones you have to hand, or add extras. The more the merrier.

SERVES 4

1 chicken breast

500ml sunflower oil, for frying

1 tablespoon of finely grated fresh ginger

3 tablespoons plain flour, sifted

1 medium egg, lightly beaten

1 large carrot, siced on the diagonal into 1–2cm rounds

2 leeks, cut into 1–2cm pieces

2 onions, cut into 2cm pieces

2 peppers, cut into 2cm pieces

2 tomatoes, cut into 2cm pieces

½ large pineapple, cut into 2cm pieces

1 tablespoon cornflour

FOR THE SWEET AND SOUR SAUCE

2 tablespoons cornflour

100ml water

4 tablespoons soft brown sugar

2 tablespoons soy sauce

6 tablespoons rice or white wine vinegar

2 tablespoons tomato ketchup

 3 OF YOUR 5 A DAY

Cut the chicken into 2.5cm cubes and place in a bowl with the ginger. Marinate for 30 minutes, or as long as overnight.

Place a deep layer of oil (10–12cm deep) in a large pot. Set over medium-high heat.

Make the batter for the chicken: sift the flour into a medium-sized bowl, drop the egg into the centre and beat until the mixture is smooth. Set aside.

Prepare the sauce: place the cornflour in a small saucepan. Mix in the water, sugar, soy sauce, vinegar and ketchup and set over a low heat. Simmer gently, stirring occasionally, until it has thickened – this should take about 3 minutes.

Dust the chicken with 1 tablespoon of cornflour then coat in the batter.

Fry the batter-coated chicken, a few pieces at a time, until golden, for about 3 minutes. Cut one piece open to check that it's cooked through. Set aside while you cook the vegetables.

Place a large wok or frying pan over high heat. Add a splash of sunflower or vegetable oil. Add the onions and carrots and stir-fry briskly for a few minutes. Add the pineapple, leeks and peppers, followed by the sauce. Bring the sauce up to a boil.

As soon as the sauce is bubbling, mix in the chicken along with the tomatoes to coat in the sauce. Serve with rice.

Chicken, coconut and butternut squash curry

Curries and other Indian dishes offer much inspiration when it comes to eating less meat and more veg. Even though Indians love their ghee, they still consume very few animal products compared to the rest of the world. In 1997, the average Indian consumed only 174 calories from animal products each day compared to the average French person, who ate 1,334 calories worth of meat, dairy and eggs on a daily basis. When you have all those beautiful spices and a rich coconut broth, you really don't need much meat to make a wonderfully satisfying meal.

SERVES 4–6

olive oil

1 butternut squash, peeled and cut into 4cm hunks

1 chicken breast or 2 thighs, cut into bite-sized pieces

1 large onion, finely chopped

sea salt

4cm piece of fresh ginger, peeled and grated

3 garlic cloves, finely chopped

1 small chilli, deseeded and finely chopped (use less for a milder curry)

1 tablespoon each of turmeric, ground cumin and ground coriander

8 cardamom pods, crushed

1 small cauliflower, cut into florets

2 courgettes, cut into 1cm rounds

800ml coconut milk

juice from ½ lime

4 tablespoons crème fraîche, or Cashew Cream, page 181

a big handful of fresh coriander, roughly chopped

❀ 2.5 OF YOUR 5 A DAY

Set a big saucepan over medium heat and add a splash of oil. When it's warm, add the squash and cook for 10 minutes. Add the chicken and onion and a pinch of salt, turn the heat up, and sizzle for a few moments. Fold in the ginger, garlic, chilli and spices. Sauté for a couple of minutes, then add the cauliflower and courgettes and fry for a few moments – try to pick up a bit of colour on the courgettes. Add a bit more oil if needed.

Stir in the coconut milk and bring to the boil. Turn down the heat, cover and simmer gently for about 10 minutes or until the veg and chicken are cooked through.

If you're serving with rice, start cooking it now.

Once the veg and chicken are cooked, fold the lime juice and crème fraîche or Cashew Cream into the sauce. Simmer for a few more minutes.

Remove from the heat. Garnish with coriander leaves and serve immediately.

VEGGIE OPTION

This dish can easily be made without meat, as all the vegetables and the rich sauce are deliciously satisfying on their own.

Mexican cold remedy
with sweet potato crisps and bread

In Mexico, the darker meat of chicken is preferred over the white. So, I've used chicken drumsticks in this heavenly Yucatan-style sopa de lima or 'lime soup'. As well as soul-warming chicken broth and meat, it's full of cold-busting vitamin C. A delicious winter remedy. The sweet potato bread and crisps make it more substantial and add a portion of veg.

SERVES 4

2 chicken drumsticks

1 small or ½ large cinnamon stick

4 allspice berries (optional)

1 litre chicken or vegetable stock

2 onions, finely chopped

2 garlic cloves, finely chopped

1 large carrot, peeled and diced

4 tomatoes, diced

pinch of red chilli, deseeded and finely chopped

splash of olive oil

juice and zest of 3 limes

juice and zest of 2 oranges

TO SERVE

2 spring onions, thinly sliced

2 handfuls of fresh coriander

1 ripe avocado

olive oil

sea salt and black pepper

3.5 OF YOUR 5 A DAY WITH THE SWEET POTATO BREAD AND CRISPS

Place the chicken drumsticks, spices and stock in a pot. Bring to the boil. Reduce heat and simmer for 20 minutes. When the chicken has cooked through, remove it and let it cool.

Meanwhile, in a large pot, sauté the onion, garlic, carrot, tomato and chilli in a splash of olive oil, until softened.

Pour the broth over the vegetables. Add the lime and orange juice and zest. Let it simmer while you shred the meat from the chicken drumsticks; add this to the soup and continue to simmer for 20 minutes.

When you're ready to serve the soup, divide among 4 bowls. Top with a handful of sweet potato crisps, spring onion slices and coriander. Serve with avocado slices and sweet potato bread, if you have time to make it.

SWEET POTATO CRISPS AND BREAD

Peel 3 sweet potatoes, then use the peeler to shave 12 long slivers from each one. Fry in a deep pot of hot sunflower oil in batches, until crisp and just golden. Finely dice the remaining sweet potato. Warm a large frying pan over medium heat. Add a splash of olive oil. Cook the sweet potatoes until really tender. Take off the heat. Mash until smooth. Add a pinch of paprika, salt and a handful of chopped coriander leaves. Dust plain white flour over the top. You want a ratio of 1 part flour to 3 parts sweet potato, or just enough to form a soft, playdough-like dough. Tip onto a floured surface and roll out until roughly 5mm thick. Cut into 6cm square-ish pieces. Cook in a dry frying pan over medium-high heat until golden on each side. Serve warm.

Finger lickin' BBQ chicken platter

Think Hard Rock Café or TGI Fridays but with a healthy, homemade twist. It's a great way to make use of chicken wings or drumsticks, which are very cheap to buy.

Seek out a good, locally-sourced beer for your onion ring batter, and a couple of extra bottles to drink. The BBQ Sauce can be made up to one week in advance and freezes well. If you're short on time, use your favourite barbecue sauce instead.

SERVES 2

4 chicken drumsticks or
8 chicken wings

500ml sunflower oil

250g plain white flour

500ml beer

4 whole corn on the cob

2–3 large onions, sliced into
1cm rings

4 medium-sized tomatoes,
halved

a handful of coriander leaves,
optional

5-MINUTE BBQ SAUCE

1 small onion or shallot, very
finely chopped

1 garlic clove, finely minced

sea salt and black pepper

olive oil

150ml ketchup

½ teaspoon fresh rosemary,
leaves finely chopped

1 teaspoon Dijon mustard

1 teaspoon soy sauce

1 teaspoon balsamic vinegar

½ teaspoon smoky paprika

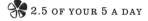 2.5 OF YOUR 5 A DAY

Preheat the oven to 220°C/gas mark 7.

To make the barbecue sauce, place a small frying pan over medium heat. Add the onion, garlic and pinch of salt. Let it cook, no oil added, for a moment to let the water cook out of the onion. When it starts to look dry, add a splash of olive oil. Stir it through and scrape the bottom of the pan (using a wooden spoon — otherwise you and your pans are in big trouble!).

Add the remaining ingredients. Let it cook for a few minutes, allowing the flavours to mingle and the sauce to thicken up a bit. Leave to cool and then rub into the meat. Coat the chicken in the barbecue sauce. Place in a lightly oiled roasting tin. Set aside.

Pop the corn in a small, lightly oiled tray. Sprinkle a bit of salt over and pop into the oven. Place the tray of chicken in the oven as well. Try to fit them both on a middle rack. If there's not room, cook the chicken higher up, with the corn sitting on a rack below. Roast the corn and chicken, turning once or twice, for 30 minutes, or until the corn kernels are tender and the chicken is cooked through.

Place the oil in a large pot and set over medium-high heat.

Place the flour in a bowl and slowly whisk in the beer until the batter is as thick as double cream.

Sift through the rings of onion and pop the larger ones in the batter, one at a time. Reserve the smaller ones to use in a soup or another dish later in the week. Try to ensure you have 7–8 big rings per person. Fry the batter-coated rings in small batches. Drain in a colander or on stale slices of bread (unwanted ends of a loaf are good for this).

Once everything is cooked, arrange on a plate or platter. Finish off each plate or the platter with the halved tomatoes and drape a few herbs over, if you like. Serve with a cold beer.

Wholesome chicken pie

A hearty and wholesome meal, with a touch of cream, loads of veg and very little chicken needed, especially if you get some delicious stock going through it. It's a great dish for any cut of chicken, be it two thighs, a leg or a breast, so is a great one for using up any meat in your freezer, or leftovers from a roast.

SERVES 6

olive oil

2 chicken thighs

500ml chicken stock or water

3 carrots, diced

2 leeks, thinly sliced

5 celery sticks, thinly sliced

3 garlic cloves, chopped

200g wild or chestnut mushrooms (see other seasonal options, below)

250ml white wine

juice and zest of 1 lemon

100ml double cream

1 tablespoon Dijon or wholegrain mustard

a handful of fresh herbs, roughly chopped

sea salt and black pepper

Pat-in-the-Pan Pastry, page 159

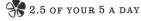 2.5 OF YOUR 5 A DAY

Add a splash of olive oil to a saucepan. Add the chicken and sauté until it starts to pick up colour. Cover with stock and simmer for 30 minutes.

Place a large frying pan over medium heat, add a little olive oil and when it's warm, add the carrots, leeks, celery and garlic. Sauté for 15–20 minutes until the veg starts to soften. Ladle in a bit of the stock from the chicken and let it sizzle to help soften the veg.

Remove the chicken from the stock, let it cool, then shred the meat and add to the vegetables. Pour in the wine and let it reduce slightly. Fold in the lemon juice and zest, double cream and mustard, and cook for a moment to thicken.

Sauté the mushrooms in olive oil until golden. Fold through the pie mixture, along with the herbs. Pile the mixture into a pie dish large enough to hold everything.

Preheat the oven to 190°C/gas mark 5.

Make the Pat-in-the-Pan Pastry, but rather than patting in the pan, roll it out. Make sure you do this on a well-floured surface, or roll it between pieces of greaseproof paper to keep it from sticking and tearing. Cover the pie with the pastry.

Bake for 30–40 minutes, or until the pastry is golden. Serve with roast potatoes and a salad.

TASTE OF THE SEASON

Instead of the mushrooms you could try broad beans (podded and slipped out of their skins) and asparagus (cut into 2cm hunks), added with the fresh herbs; or pumpkin, parsnips or swede (peeled and diced), added with the carrots, leeks and celery.

Succulent roast duck
with cherry sauce and roast potatoes

Duck is up to 5 per cent richer in iron than chicken and the meat itself is surprisingly lean. If you roast the bird nicely, most of the fat (which is good for you anyway) melts down to make a wonderful coating for roast potatoes. You'll then have extra fat to render down for pastry or even more crispy, flavoursome spuds. Do give this one a go.

SERVES 4

1kg potatoes, peeled and cut into chunks

1 whole duck (about 2kg)

350g cherries, pitted

1 star anise or a cinnamon stick

2–3 teaspoons sea salt

300ml dessert wine, or a luscious red wine

2 teaspoons caster sugar, if needed

❀ THE SAUCE ALONE PROVIDES 1 OF YOUR 5 A DAY, SERVE WITH A SIDE OF VEG TO INCREASE THIS TO 2.5

NOTE if fresh cherries are out of season, used roughly the same weight of frozen or a jar of preserved cherries. You can also use 75g dried sour cherries — try to get the natural, unsweetened ones.

Preheat the oven to 220°C/gas mark 7.

Arrange the potatoes in a roasting tin.

Pack the cherries and cinnamon or star anise into the cavity of the duck. Pat the skin of the duck dry – this will help crisp the skin. Prick the skin all over, getting right down through the fat and to the flesh. Rub the salt all over the bird. Place the duck breast-side down onto the potatoes. Cook for 45 minutes with the bird on its breasts.

Turn the oven down to 200°C/gas mark 6. Take the roasting tin out and carefully flip the duck breast-side up. Continue roasting for another 20–35 minutes.

Pierce a fat bit of the leg to see if the juices that run from it are clear; if so, the duck is cooked. If not, cook for a bit longer and if the skin is getting too dark, just loosely cover it with foil until you get clear juices.

Transfer the duck to a serving plate or board, one that will catch any juices. Spoon the potatoes into a serving dish. Strain the fat from the pan into a glass jar (an old jam jar works well).

Spoon the cherries and cinnamon stick or star anise out of the duck's cavity and put them back into the pan. Add 2 tablespoons of the fat you've just strained off. Pour the wine in, place over medium heat and let it bubble up and reduce by about a third. Taste as it bubbles and adjust the seasoning. Add sugar if needed.

Carve the meat from the duck breasts and legs. Serve with the sauce, potatoes and sides of your choice.

Dealing with the duck carcass

After you've eaten your dinner and had a few glasses of wine and a pudding, pluck any remaining meat from the duck. There should be a good handful of meat left for the Crispy Duck Salad, page 113. Check the wings, all along the back, around the neck and so on. If you don't fancy doing this straight away, just wrap the duck up and do it the next day. The cooked duck (once removed from the bone) will keep in the fridge for up to 4 days.

TO MAKE CRISPY DUCK CRACKLING

Even if you served some of the skin with your roast, you should have some left to refrigerate. It will go soft in the fridge but as soon as you fry it in a bit of oil or duck fat, it will crisp back up. It makes the most delicious croûtons for the Star Anise Broth (see page 112), Crispy Duck Salad (see page 113) or any other salad for that matter.

TO RENDER DUCK FAT

Chop up and render out any remaining skin. This will give you a deliciously creamy duck fat — just the sort you'd buy in the supermarket for roast potatoes. Think of it as butter, as both are animal fats in the end.

Preheat the oven to 150°C/gas mark 2. Roughly chop the fat into 1–2cm pieces. Place in a small, ovenproof pot with a lid. Put it in the oven for 45 minutes to 1 hour, or longer if you can. The longer you leave it, the more you'll get.

This fat makes great roast potatoes. You can also use it instead of beef dripping in the pastry on page 26.

JEWISH POPCORN

In traditional Jewish cooking, the skin from poultry is never wasted. After roasting the bird, the skin is crisped up in the oven and eaten as a snack called grebenes or 'Jewish Popcorn'.

TO MAKE A QUICK DUCK STOCK

Use the bones to make a quick stock for the Star Anise Broth, which is basically noodles in a rich stock with any veggies you'd like to add.

To make the stock, place the duck bones in a pot (use the same one you made the gravy in, not washing beforehand) and you'll pick up some of those lovely spiced cherry flavours in your stock. Add 1–2 quartered onions, a few black peppercorns, the cinnamon stick or star anise you popped into the cavity of the roast duck and 2–3 carrots halved lengthwise.

Pour enough water into the pot to just cover the bones. Pop a lid on and bring to the boil, reduce the heat slightly and let it bubble away for 30 minutes. Turn the heat off and let it infuse as it cools.

Strain the veg and bones out and pour the stock into pots or jars that you can store in the fridge or freezer. If you have the time and inclination, you can reduce the stock by one-third for a richer, fuller flavour.

Star anise broth

I love making this dish. I normally start making the stock for it soon after I've eaten my roast duck so I can throw the bones into the gravy pot. This means you get an extra layer of flavour.

SERVES 4

1 litre duck stock (see page 111)

1-2 star anise

200g brown rice or buckwheat noodles

200g fresh or frozen peas

200g pak choi or spinach, roughly chopped

½ cucumber, sliced into matchsticks

12 spring onions, sliced into rounds or matchsticks

a little dried chilli

a splash of soy sauce

sea salt and black pepper

a handful of crispy duck crackling (see page 111), optional

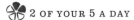 2 OF YOUR 5 A DAY

Warm the stock with the star anise. Add the noodles and cook until tender. Stir the remaining ingredients through. Add a splash of soy sauce and a grinding of pepper. Finish with crispy duck crackling, if you like.

Crispy duck salad

In my mind, crispy duck skin is as tasty as pork crackling. In this dish, you get a real taste for the Chinese restaurant classic: crispy duck and pancakes. It's so satisfying to make your own version, and it's really easy once you've roasted your duck.

SERVES 4

8 plums

½ teaspoon ground Sichuan peppercorns

½ teaspoon ground cloves

½ teaspoon ground fennel seeds

4 star anise

½ teaspoon cinnamon stick or ¼ teaspoon ground cinnamon

½ teaspoon grated fresh ginger

½ teaspoon red chilli, roughly chopped

2 tablespoons soy sauce

1½ tablespoons demerara sugar

4 tablespoons duck fat

1 cucumber, cut into matchsticks

12 spring onions, cut into 4cm-long pieces and shredded

200g leftover roast duck meat, shredded

crispy duck crackling (see page 111)

sea salt

100g mixed salad leaves or crispy baby gem lettuce

1 lime (optional)

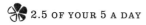 2.5 OF YOUR 5 A DAY

Cut the plums in half and remove the stones. Place the plums, spices, soy sauce, sugar and duck fat in a large, lidded saucepan or frying pan — one that will allow the plums to sit in a single layer. Mix all the ingredients well.

Place the pan over medium-high heat and let it warm to where it just starts to bubble up. Pop a lid on, turn down the heat and let the spiced plums simmer for 15–20 minutes or until the plums are just about to fall apart. The plum juices should have seeped out and enriched the sauce, which you'll use as a dressing over the duck and the salad.

Prepare the cucumber and spring onions while you wait for the plums to cook.

Use a slotted spoon to remove the plums from the pan. Set aside. Place the leftover duck meat in the plum sauce and let it warm through.

Warm a small frying pan over high heat. Add the duck skin and let it sizzle until golden. Sprinkle a tiny bit of sea salt over and spoon into a sieve or onto a piece of stale bread (I usually save the heel end of a loaf for this) to drain any excess fat.

Arrange the salad leaves in the centre of the plate. Dot 4 plums around them. Scatter the spring onions and cucumber around. Pile the saucy meat in the centre and sprinkle the crispy skin over the top. Spritz a bit of lime juice over the top, if you like, and serve.

VEG PATCH

Calorie for calorie, spinach has more protein than a cheeseburger. Gram for gram, watercress has more calcium than milk. Fruits and vegetables have so much to give. According to the World Cancer Research Fund, a healthy plate is one that is at least two thirds full of such plants.

Very few of us, however, manage to eat anywhere near enough. This chapter is here to inspire you to spoon a few more vegetables onto your plate. It's also designed to encourage you to eat seasonal produce. A Japanese study showed that foods grown in their correct season can contain up to three times more nutrients than when they're grown out of season.

As well as seeking seasonal vegetables, try to source ones that are grown near you. Food that's local to you is both seasonally relevant and it's fresher.

Only one in five children eat their '5 A Day'. The World Cancer Research Fund warns that this could increase the risk of developing cancer because they don't get enough of the vitamins and nutrients found in fruit and vegetables.

Local food also tastes nicer because it can be picked when it's perfectly ripe and nutritionally at its best. This makes it satisfying on a much deeper level. Consider supporting the local economy as well and it all adds up.

Now, I know that a lot of people are sceptical about organic food and think that it's overpriced, posh food for the middle classes. It can be more expensive. But there's a reason why: it's grown more slowly and with more care. Furthermore, you get more nutritional benefit for your money; stacks of studies show that organic food to be richer in minerals and vitamins. I work in the organic sector, so you could say I'm biased, but this has given me a much greater insight to its true virtues. It's so much more than food that is free of pesticides. While this is certainly a positive thing, what really inspires me is that organic food comes from soil that is teeming with life and minerals.

Intensive agriculture not only relies on chemicals to keep wildlife from eating their crops, but it is also dependent on fertilisers. Intensification of commercial horticulture means the goodness is literally used up. The soil is basically flatlining and needs artificial stimulants.

You can feel the difference if you pick up a handful of earth from an organic patch versus soil from a conventional field. I've seen the difference between the soils under a microscope. Organic soils are rich with earthworms and other microscopic forms of life wiggling their way through the earth, driving oxygen in through their pathways and giving the roots of the plants we eat greater scope to dig deeper and draw in more goodness.

Some organic farmers will say they don't farm fruit, vegetables or animals but they farm the soil. This is where all the essential minerals and nutrients we need come from. Healthy soil = healthy plants = healthy people.

Organic crops had significantly higher levels of all 21 nutrients analysed compared with conventional produce including vitamin C (27 per cent more), magnesium (29 per cent more), iron (21 per cent more) and phosphorous (14 per cent more).

UK and US government statistics indicate that levels of trace minerals in fruit and vegetables fell by up to 76 per cent between 1940 and 1991.

Saffron asparagus

SERVES 4

350g asparagus, woody ends trimmed

1 lemon, juice and zest

pinch of saffron strands

olive oil

sea salt and black pepper

Steam or cook the asparagus in a shallow pool of boiling water until just tender. Drain the water. Return to the warm pan. Toss with the lemon juice and zest, saffron and a little bit of olive oil. Season well. Serve.

 1 OF YOUR 5 A DAY

Sweet balsamic beetroot with a hint of chilli

SERVES 4

2–3 beetroot, peeled and cut in 1cm slices

a slice of red chilli, finely chopped

1 teaspoon honey

a few splashes of balsamic vinegar

fresh mint, tarragon or parsley

olive oil

sea salt and black pepper

Place a large, lidded frying pan over high heat. Splash a bit of olive oil into the pan. When hot, arrange the beetroot slices across the bottom in a single, but slightly overlapping (if needed) layer.

Pop a lid on, turn down the heat and let them sizzle and sweat for 10–15 minutes, just until they start to soften up. Take the lid off.

Add the chilli and a bit more oil, if needed. Sauté for a moment. Season. Shuffle it through. Drizzle the honey over and a good splash of balsamic. Stir through. Let it reduce right down, giving the beets a nice sweet coating.

Take off the heat, sprinkle with herbs and they're ready to serve.

 1 OF YOUR 5 A DAY

Broad beans with lemon, basil and pine nuts

SERVES 4

1kg broad beans, podded

sea salt and black pepper

olive oil

juice and zest of 1 lemon

4 tablespoons pine nuts, toasted

a little pinch of chilli powder or fresh red chilli (optional)

a handful of basil, leaves torn

Get a little pot of boiling water on the go. Pop the broad beans in for a minute or two. Drain. Run under cold water to cool them down and then pop the lime green beans out of their skins. If the beans are young and small, however, you can leave the skin on.

Season the warm broad beans. Toss with a splash of olive oil, lemon juice and zest, pinenuts and chilli, if using. Scatter basil over the top and serve.

 1 OF YOUR 5 A DAY

Broccoli with toasted almonds

SERVES 4

4 tablespoons flaked almonds

sea salt and black pepper

350g purple sprouting or regular broccoli, cut into florets and stalks trimmed and sliced into 1cm thick rounds

juice and zest of 1 orange or lemon

olive oil

Place a frying pan over high heat. Add the almonds, turn down the heat and gently toast until just golden. Sprinkle with salt and tip into a bowl.

Steam or lightly boil the broccoli until tender – this takes only 3–4 minutes. Drain.

Place the orange or lemon juice in a pan with a splash of olive oil, the zest and a pinch of salt. Let the juice bubble up and reduce down a bit. Add the broccoli and toss. Season with pepper. Scatter toasted almonds over the top. Serve.

 1 OF YOUR 5 A DAY

Honey spiced cauliflower

SERVES 4

olive oil

1 small head cauliflower, sliced into 1cm panels, stalks trimmed

½ teaspoon ground cumin

½ teaspoon ground coriander

a pinch of chilli powder

1 tablespoon honey

1 lemon

a handful of fresh coriander or parsley, leaves chopped

sea salt and black pepper

Heat a good splash of olive oil in a lidded pan. Add the cauliflower, cover and cook for 3–5 minutes until softened. Dust the spices over and sauté. Drizzle the honey and lemon juice over, and toss to coat. Finish with a handful of fresh herbs.

NOTE: you can also make use of the leafy greens surrounding your cauliflower. Thinly slice and sauté them with cumin seeds in a bit of olive oil and a good pinch of sea salt. Delicious with sausages and roasted butternut squash mash.

 1 OF YOUR 5 A DAY

Earthy cumin carrots

SERVES 4–6

3–4 carrots

4 tablespoons water

½ teaspoon cumin seeds

sea salt and black pepper

Peel the carrots then halve lengthwise and cut into long, 3cm hunks. Place in a frying pan in a single layer. Add the water, a pinch of salt and pepper and cover. Place over medium heat and cook for 10 minutes, or until tender.
  Shake the pan a few times to prevent the carrots sticking and splash a bit more water in if needed. Once they've softened, remove the lid, and add a splash of olive oil to the pan, along with the cumin seeds. Fry for a minute until fragrant. Serve.

 1 OF YOUR 5 A DAY

Lemon courgettes with pine nuts

SERVES 4

2–3 courgettes

olive oil

sea salt and black pepper

juice and zest of 1 lemon

a small pinch of ground cinnamon

2 tablespoons pine nuts, toasted

Cut each courgette into three chunky pieces and quarter each one. Place a frying pan over medium heat. Add a splash of oil. When hot, add the courgettes. Season. Fry them until they start to pick up some colour. Add the lemon juice and zest, and the cinnamon. Cook until the lemon juice is pretty much absorbed and evaporated. Tip into a serving dish and top with pine nuts.

 1 OF YOUR 5 A DAY

Caramelised fennel steaks

SERVES 4

1 large or 2 small fennel

olive oil

Slice the fennel bulb into four 1cm-thick panels. Place a large frying pan over high heat. Add a splash of olive oil. Fry the slices until they are tender and have picked up a nice bit of colour, about 15 minutes.

 0.5 OF YOUR 5 A DAY

Green beans with black olives

SERVES 4

350g fine green beans, topped and tailed

1 lemon, juice and zest

3–4 tablespoons black olives, pitted and roughly chopped

a handful of flat-leaf parsley, chopped

olive oil

sea salt and black pepper

Cook the green beans in a little water until just tender. Season. Toss with a splash of olive oil, lemon juice and zest, olives and parsley. Serve.

 1 OF YOUR 5 A DAY

Griddled leeks

SERVES 4

2 large or 4 smaller leeks

olive oil

sea salt and black pepper

Trim the tops from the leeks and cut most of the dark green bits off (use them for stock). Halve along the length of each leek. Carefully rinse and brush off dirt then dry.

Place a large frying pan over medium-high heat. Add a splash of olive oil. Place the halves cut side down. Press them down with a smaller-sized lid or pan to help them caramelise and sweat a bit so they cook through. Serve.

 0.5 OF YOUR 5 A DAY

Honey mustard parsnips

SERVES 4

olive or sunflower oil

6 parsnips, peeled and cut into batons

2 teaspoons honey

1½ teaspoons wholegrain mustard

Heat a large frying pan over medium-high heat. Add a splash of oil and, when it's hot, add the parsnips. Coat in the oil and pop a lid on the pan (or cover it with another pan) and cook until the parsnips are tender, 10–15 minutes.

Remove the lid and continue to cook the parsnips until golden. Add the honey and mustard and coat. Remove from the heat and serve.

 1 OF YOUR 5 A DAY

Peas and spring onions and lemon curls

SERVES 4

350g garden peas, fresh or frozen

6 spring onions or 1 leek

olive oil

zest and juice of 1 lemon

sea salt and black pepper

a handful of fresh mint and/or basil, leaves stacked, rolled and thinly sliced

Cook the peas in a little water just until tender. Drain and set aside.

Slice the spring onions into 1cm thick rounds or thinly slice the white and green parts of a washed leek. Use a vegetable peeler to cut thin curls of zest from the lemon; you want about 3 long strips. Slice this into very thin strips.

Place a frying pan over medium heat. Add a splash of olive oil. When it's warm, sauté the spring onion or leek with the lemon zest and a pinch of salt and pepper. Cook just until softened.

Add the peas and lemon juice. Toss through and cook just until warm. Scatter herbs over the top and serve.

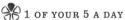 1 OF YOUR 5 A DAY

Wilted spinach and mushrooms

SERVES 4

olive oil

160g mushrooms, sliced (or torn into bite-sized pieces if wild)

160g spinach

3 garlic cloves, finely chopped

sea salt and black pepper

Heat a large frying pan over medium-high heat. Add a splash of olive oil. Add the mushrooms and cook until golden. Add the garlic and cook for a few minutes more. Pile all the spinach on top. Place a lid over the pan, cramming the spinach down in there and let it wilt for a minute or two. Remove the lid and fold the spinach through. Season with salt and pepper. Fold it all together and serve.

 1 OF YOUR 5 A DAY

Tomatoes with capers and mint

SERVES 4

500g fresh cherry or smaller plum tomatoes, halved (try a colourful mix of heirloom varieties)

1 tablespoon capers

a handful of fresh mint, leaves stacked, rolled and thinly sliced

olive oil

sea salt and black pepper

Sprinkle a bit of salt and pepper over the tomatoes then drizzle over some olive oil. Scatter the capers on top and mix. Finish with a dusting of mint. Serve.

 1.5 OF YOUR 5 A DAY

SLOW-COOKED VEGETABLE SIDES

Red cabbage braised in balsamic vinegar

SERVES 4–6

½ red cabbage

a splash of olive oil

75ml balsamic vinegar

1 tablespoon caster sugar

2 tablespoons water

sea salt and black pepper

Finely shred the cabbage, discarding the white core. Place into a heavy-based pot over a low heat with the oil, vinegar, sugar and water. Simmer with the lid on. Cook over a very low heat for about 1 hour, stirring from time to time, adding a little water if necessary to make sure it doesn't dry out on the bottom of the pot. The cabbage is ready when it releases its natural sugars and is nice and tender. Season to taste.

 1 OF YOUR 5 A DAY

Sticky orange-glazed shallots

SERVES 4–6

12 small shallots

a splash of olive oil

juice and zest of 1 orange,

1 teaspoon brown sugar, honey or maple syrup

Trim the root-end off each shallot and snip any stringy bits off the tail-end. Place snugly (but in a single layer) in a roasting dish. Drizzle a bit of oil over. Place in a hot 200°C/gas mark 6 oven. They'll take about an hour to soften up so if you're cooking them to go with roast beef, cook them at the same time.

Once their skins look a bit loose and the shallots are tender when squeezed, use two forks to carefully pull them out of their skins. Place them back in the dish with the orange juice, zest and brown sugar and let them cook further until the juice is thick and sticky. If you're pressed for time, you can do this last bit (i.e. cooking them in the juice and sugar until sticky) in a frying pan on the hob.

 1 OF YOUR 5 A DAY

I've made these to serve one person, as this is the sort of soup you (or at least I) would whip up when hungry and home alone. They're faster than ordering a take-away, are tremendously good for you, and they taste damn good. As a bonus, all are completely dairy-free. Scale up to serve more.

Pea, mint and pine nut soup

Pine nuts give the soup a luxuriously creamy texture and the mint makes it taste like a bowlful of spring.

SERVES 1

120g frozen or fresh peas

1 garlic clove, peeled

175ml chicken stock or water

2 tablespoons pine nuts, toasted

1 tablespoon olive oil

a handful of fresh mint leaves

sea salt and pepper

🍀 1.5 OF YOUR 5 A DAY

Place the peas, garlic and stock in a saucepan. Bring to the boil. Turn off the heat and let it sit for 3 minutes.

Grind the pine nuts to a paste in a blender or with a pestle and mortar. Trickle in the olive oil and give it a good mix.

Place the peas in a blender with the pine nut paste and fresh mint. Whizz to a smooth purée. Add more stock if needed. If you want a smoother soup, pass it through a sieve. Season to taste and serve.

Tomato miso ginger soup

This one hits the spot on so many levels. It's a great one to sup if you need to blast a cold.

SERVES

4 tomatoes, quartered

1 garlic clove, peeled

olive oil

100ml chicken stock or water

freshly ground black pepper

1 teaspoon miso (any will do, I usually opt for brown rice miso)

½ teaspoon fresh ginger, grated

 A WHOPPING 4 OF YOUR 5 A DAY

Pop the tomatoes and garlic in a food-processor or blender. Blitz to a smooth purée.

Place the puréed tomatoes in a frying pan with a splash of olive oil, stock and a pinch of pepper. Cook over medium-high heat for 5–10 minutes, until the mixture has thickened up and most of the water from the tomatoes has evaporated.

Stir in the miso and ginger. Warm through for a minute and then whizz in a blender until smooth.

You can pass this through a sieve to remove the tomato seeds and skin if you like but I don't bother. It tastes great either way.

Spiced sweet potato soup

Thick, wholesome and warming – like a hand-knitted jumper.

SERVES 1

olive oil

1 sweet potato, peeled and cut into 1cm dice

a pinch each of ground cinnamon and chilli

6 Brazil nuts or 10 cashew nuts

1 garlic clove, peeled

300–500ml chicken or vegetable stock

sea salt and black pepper

 2 OF YOUR 5 A DAY

Place a large frying pan over medium-high heat. Add a good glug of olive oil.

When hot, stir the sweet potato through the oil. Add the cinnamon and chilli. Pop a lid on and cook for 10 minutes, stirring occasionally. It's done when you can mash the sweet potato with the back of a spoon.

While it cooks, grind the nuts with the garlic clove until you have a fairly smooth paste. Add a splash of olive oil, if needed.

Stir the nutty garlic paste into the sweet potato and cook for a minute. Pour in just enough stock to wet it. Let it bubble up to warm through.

Whizz in a blender until smooth, adding more stock if needed. Press through a sieve if you want a smoother texture. Slurp while it's warm.

A guide to salads

A few fantastic ways to cut your veg...

CHOP

Chopped salads have tremendous crunch and flavour. The idea is to chop all of your salad ingredients into a similar-sized dice, so in each mouthful you have a mix of different veggies throwing off all sorts of wonderful flavours. Classic chopped salads include the Cobb and the Waldorf.

Throw a few surprises into the mix, such as toasted nuts, seeds, chickpeas, croûtons or fried onions.

Turn a chopped medley into a main course by adding shreds of leftover meat, boiled egg, cheese or fish. You can also stuff a chopped salad into pita bread or fold it into a warm tortilla wrap.

GRATE

This is a brilliant way to get winter roots into a salad. Beetroot, celeriac, parsnips, carrots add delicious crunch and colour. Firm apples and pears also work well in the mix. My favourite winter salad is grated raw beetroot and apple with toasted walnuts and Chilli Balsamic Vinaigrette (page 127). I serve this on a mound of leaves with ripe pear slices and a crumbling of blue cheese.

JULIENNE

You don't need a special mandolin to do this. I just use a wide knife blade and a cutting board. That's it. Just peel your vegetables, if needed. Slice into 0.5cm-thick panels (or as thin as you can slice them). Then cut each panel into matchsticks — the length (and width) is up to you.

Perfect julienne veg include: carrots, courgettes, celeriac, beetroot, butternut squash, cucumbers, Jerusalem artichokes and kohlrabi. Apples and pears are also delicious in salads this way.

RIBBONS AND SHAVINGS

Any fairly firm vegetable can be cut into long ribbons or wispy shavings with a vegetable peeler. Just approach it as though you're going to peel it but keep going beyond the peel (if it has one).

Ribbons: courgettes, cucumber, carrots, broccoli stalks and butternut squash (it softens and effectively cooks in a vinaigrette, so don't be afraid to use it in salads).

Shavings: beetroot, fennel, celeriac, Jerusalem artichokes, kohlrab and radish.

....AND THE LEBANESE LAZY SALAD APPROACH

This is my favourite as it involves no work and it looks stunning. Children love it too. Basically, all you do is fill a salad bowl full of raw, uncut or roughly cut salad ingredients: a leafy head of lettuce, whole tomatoes, a whole cucumber, a bunch of radishes. It's a cross between a salad and crudités. If you go to a Lebanese restaurant, this is what they lay on the table before your meal. It's great.

5 KNOCKOUT **SALAD DRESSINGS**

Dijon vinaigrette

This is delicious over a simple salad of crunchy leaves, with maybe some crunchy raw peas and radishes thrown in. You can also use it to dress warm green beans.

SERVES 4–6

1 tablespoon Dijon mustard

2 tablespoons red wine vinegar

75ml olive oil (or try it with hazelnut oil – even better!)

Place all the ingredients in a jam jar. Shake and store in the fridge for up to 1 week.

Chilli balsamic vinaigrette

Stunning with beetroot, drizzled over steamed or grilled asparagus or pan-fried or raw courgette.

SERVES 4–6

4 tablespoons olive oil

2 tablespoons balsamic vinegar

2 tablespoons lime or orange juice

1 tablespoon honey

1 teaspoon soy sauce

1 chilli, halved and deseeded

Place all the ingredients in a jam jar. Shake and store in the fridge for up to 1 week.

Honey mustard thyme

Gorgeous with a simple salad of grated carrots or crunchy leaves.

SERVES 4–6

4 tablespoons olive oil

3 tablespoons grainy or Dijon mustard

2 tablespoons honey

½ garlic clove, finely minced

2 teaspoons fresh thyme leaves

sea salt and black pepper

Place all the ingredients in a jam jar. Whisk to fully mix in the honey. Store in the fridge for up to 1 week.

Summer herb vinaigrette

Lovely with summer courgettes, cut into ribbons, radishes, crunchy lettuce leaves, green beans, and more.

SERVES 4–6

a large handful of fresh, soft green herbs (e.g. basil, coriander, mint, tarragon, chives), finely chopped

100ml olive oil

3 tablespoons cider or white wine vinegar

zest of 1 lemon

1 teaspoon honey

sea salt and black pepper

Place all the ingredients in a jam jar. Shake and store in the fridge for 1–2 days.

Sesame ginger lime

This is lovely on a salad of crunchy leaves with hunks of sweet mango, freshly grated coconut, toasted cashew or macadamia nuts and fresh coriander leaves. You can also use it to dress warm carrots, beans or peas.

SERVES 4–6

125ml sesame oil

4 tablespoons lime juice

1 tablespoon honey

1 tablespoon soy sauce

3cm piece of fresh ginger, peeled and finely chopped

Place all the ingredients in a jam jar. Shake and store in the fridge for up to 1 week.

Autumn squash and sage mash

Delicious with roast chicken or lamb.

SERVES 4

1 pumpkin or squash

3–4 tablespoons olive oil

2 garlic cloves, roasted or
chopped and sautéed

4 sage leaves, finely chopped

sea salt and black pepper

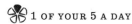 1 OF YOUR 5 A DAY

Halve and de-seed the squash. Place on a roasting tray with a little olive oil rubbed into the cavity. Roast for 45 minutes to 1 hour, until very soft. Scoop out, mix with garlic, sage and more olive oil. Season to taste. Serve, refrigerate for 2–3 days or freeze.

Creamy cannellini mash

*This one is delicious with lamb, beef or fish – try it as a winter side for the
Tandoori Spiced Black Bream, page 144.*

SERVES 4

4 tablespoon olive oil

2 garlic cloves, roughly
chopped

a handful of curly kale, finely
chopped (about 4 tablespoons)

sea salt and freshly ground
pepper

800g tinned cannellini beans,
drained (reserve 3–4
tablespoons of the liquid)

juice and zest of 1 lemon

a pinch of chilli powder

1.5 OF YOUR 5 A DAY

Place a large pan over medium heat. Add a good splash of olive oil. Add the garlic and kale and let it cook until the garlic is softened and the kale is bright green and glossy. Season well, tip out of the pan and set aside.

Place the beans in the pan with a splash of oil, salt, pepper and the lemon juice and zest. Let it warm through. Add the reserved bean juices.

Tip the beans into a food-processor with a pinch of chilli powder. Pulse until you have a thick mash. Fold the garlic and kale through. Loosen with a drizzle of olive oil or a drop of warm water, if needed. Serve.

Roasted garlic mash with kale

This one is delicious with just about everything, especially the roast pork loin on page 72.

SERVES 4

4–5 medium-sized potatoes

sea salt and black pepper

4 garlic cloves, unpeeled

2 sprigs of rosemary (optional)

6 tablespoons kale, finely chopped like parsley

olive oil or dripping

✿ 0.5 OF YOUR 5 A DAY

Wash your potatoes, prick all over with a fork and place in a dish. Sprinkle 1–2 tablespoons sea salt over the potatoes — this draws out moisture from the potatoes and gives you a fluffy, full-flavoured mash. Add the garlic cloves alongside and some rosemary, if you like. Place in the oven and roast until tender.

Check the garlic cloves from time to time and remove them as soon as they're soft enough to squeeze – they'll be ready before the potatoes (after 30–40 minutes cooking).

Remove the potato and garlic from their skins and mash together. Sauté the kale in a warm frying pan with a little oil and a pinch of salt, just until glossy and bright green. Fold through the mash and serve.

Pear and celeriac mash

Stunning with roast pork or chicken.

SERVES 4

olive oil

1 celeriac, peeled and cut into 1–2cm dice

2 garlic cloves, chopped

2 pears, peeled, cored and diced

juice and zest of 1 lemon

a few sprigs of rosemary, leaves finely chopped

sea salt and black pepper

✿ 1.5 OF YOUR 5 A DAY

Place a large pot over medium heat. Add a good splash of olive oil. When hot, add the celeriac. Stir through the oil, then pop a lid on and turn the heat down. Sauté for 20 minutes, or until completely tender and starting to caramelise. Stir occasionally.

Season. Add the garlic and pear. Sauté for 5–10 minutes until tender. Add the lemon juice and let it sizzle up.

Tip everything into a food-processor (including the lemon zest and rosemary). Whizz until smooth. Add a touch more olive oil and/or water to soften and loosen up, if needed. Season. If you don't have a food-processor, just mash everything until smooth and well combined. Serve warm.

GAME

Modern farming results in a less varied and less balanced diet than hunting and gathering achieves.

We eat only a tiny percentage of the food available to us. One of the reasons for this is the growth of towns and cities. They have disconnected us from nature. Our food choices are now presented to us on supermarket shelves instead of in forests, fields and hedgerows. If you leaf through old cookbooks you'll see a feast of foods that are no longer part of our diets.

I have a reprint of a marvellous book by Alexis Soyer, a flamboyant French chef whose gastronomic genius was all the rage when Queen Victoria was on the throne. The book was first published in 1853 and, incredibly, features recipes for more than 30 types of game. Alexis' book includes the more familiar pheasant, partridge, quail, rabbit and deer. But also featured are thrush, blackbird, starling, wood-hen, bustard, teal, woodcock, snipe, curlew, lark, squirrel, fox and dozens more.

Your grandparents would have dined on game (and offal) regularly. Until the 1950s, rabbit was more commonly eaten than chicken. Eating squirrel was not unusual when my granny was a young girl. The reason we're so squeamish about these meats is not because they taste funny. When my mom first had rabbit as a child she proclaimed: 'This is the best chicken I've ever eaten.' We're just not used to seeing game in the shops, and the variety on restaurant menus is often limiting. We should certainly eat more of them.

Wood pigeons are probably the most plentiful wild bird. They take minutes to cook and taste delicious as a result of their foraged diet.

Our food culture seems to get narrower and narrower, despite all the perceived choice, and this is certainly to the detriment of our health and the environment. Eating game can broaden your diet in so many ways.

When buying game such as venison, rabbit, partridge and so on, try to go for the wild versions. Wild game is richer in taste and nutritional benefits. It is leaner than farmed animals, because they are typically more active.

If you cannot source wild game, there are some very good game farmers who rear their animals outdoors and feed them a natural diet of grass and vegetables. However, you can also get some very badly farmed game. Some rabbits are reared in conditions not dissimilar from those endured by factory farmed chickens. These rabbits are housed in cages, with little natural light or fresh air. They are also fed man-made pellets rather than the food nature intended for them.

As with all the meat you buy, find out the story behind it – where it came from, what sort of life the animal lived and, most importantly, what it ate. At the end of the day, this translates into the food you'll be eating.

Tuscan rabbit with balsamic tomatoes and thyme

Rabbit is an extremely popular meat throughout Italy. There's a rabbit dish for nearly every Italian region. I tried a good few when trying to lay my hands on a really simple, tasty rabbit dish that anyone can whip up, especially if you've never cooked with rabbit before.

The best place to source rabbit is from a farmers' market or a good local butcher. It's not always on display, though. If you don't see it, ask – noting that you're after wild rabbit. Good butchers normally have some to hand, or they can get some for you. It's well worth seeking out.

SERVES 4

2 rabbit portions (see box)

plain white flour, for dusting

olive oil

2 onions, chopped

4 garlic cloves, finely chopped

sea salt and black pepper

650g tomatoes, roughly chopped

½ teaspoon turmeric (optional)

1 teaspoon fennel seeds

a sprig of rosemary, leaves finely chopped

6 tablespoons balsamic vinegar

a few sprigs of thyme

🍀 2.5 OF YOUR 5 A DAY

Preheat the oven to 180°C/gas mark 4.

Season the rabbit and dust with flour, just enough to lightly coat it.

Place a frying pan over medium-high heat. Add a splash of olive oil. When hot, carefully add the rabbit portions. Cook until golden, 5–8 minutes on each side. Once browned, place snugly in a baking dish.

Clean your frying pan then place back on the heat. Add a splash of oil. When hot, toss the onion and garlic in the pan and fry with a pinch of salt until translucent, about 5 minutes. Add the tomatoes, turmeric, fennel seeds and rosemary. Cook until the tomatoes start to soften up. Add half the balsamic vinegar and let it bubble and reduce into the tomatoes for a few minutes.

Pour over the rabbit. Tuck a few sprigs of thyme on the top. Cook, uncovered, for 20 minutes. Splash the remaining balsamic on top. Continue cooking for 15–20 minutes, until the tomato sauce looks rich and thick. Let it cool for a moment. Remove the rabbit. Carefully shred the meat, removing it from thebone, and fold through the sauce.

Serve with hunks of bread and a crisp salad — and a nice glass of wine.

USING THE WHOLE RABBIT

Ask your butcher to cut the rabbit for you — you should get six pieces: two hind legs, the front legs, and two central pieces. The larger, hind legs are ideal for this dish.

Use the meatier central piece for kebabs — freeze the hunks of meat and skewer as part of a mixed grill; rabbit works well with Guinness Mustard Marinade, page 64. Use a smaller central piece and the smaller hind leg pieces to make soup and stock - try Rabbit Risotto Soup, page 134.

Rabbit risotto soup

Thick, rich and creamy – just like a risotto but with a touch more stock. It's a delicious way to sample the tender meat of rabbit in a familiar setting. You could also make this with chicken or lamb.

SERVES 4

a splash of olive oil

1 onion, finely chopped

2 carrots, finely diced

175g risotto rice

1.2 litres rabbit stock, below

150g cooked rabbit, shredded

300g frozen peas, defrosted

juice and zest of 1 lemon

1 tablespoon Dijon mustard

a handful of tarragon, basil and/or thyme, chopped

 2 OF YOUR 5 A DAY

Place a frying pan over medium heat. Add a splash of olive oil. When hot, add the onion and carrots. Cook until they're nicely softened.

Add the risotto rice to the pan and stir to coat in olive oil. Set a timer for 20 minutes. Slowly ladle in the stock, stirring frequently until the timer goes off. Add the shredded rabbit and a final ladle or two of stock, to make the rice soupy.

Purée half the peas in a food-processor. Add them to the soup, along with the remaining whole peas, lemon juice and zest and mustard. Cook for 5 minutes longer.

Season to taste. Serve with a smattering of herbs on top.

RABBIT STOCK

Rabbit stock is easy to make. Just place two pieces of a jointed rabbit — ideally the front legs (they'll look a bit like chicken thighs on the bone). The meat will cook as you make your stock, which makes the soup above ideal as you can use the tender meat and the stock all in one go.

TO MAKE Place a saucepan over medium-high heat. Add a splash of olive oil. Fry the rabbit until it picks up a bit of colour. Add a quartered onion, a roughly chopped carrot, a few peppercorns and a handful of herbs. Fry them for a moment.

Top with 1.5 litres of water and bring to the boil. Turn down the heat and simmer for 30 minutes.

Strain the stock off, gently pressing the veg to extract as much flavour as possible. Take out the meat. Cool and shred it. Add the stock and meat to the risotto soup, above, or try it instead of chicken in the Italian Chicken Soup, page 99.

Winter wood pigeon salad

Wood pigeon is great, fast to cook and has an incredible flavour that sits somewhere between beef and chicken. That may sound a little odd but wood pigeon meat is meaty like a steak yet soft and tender like a chicken breast. Give it a go and you'll see what I mean. Wood pigeon take literally about 5 minutes to cook.

SERVES 4

2 pomegranates

4 oranges

1 garlic clove, finely chopped

sea salt and black pepper

4 wood pigeon breasts

olive oil

1 sprig of rosemary

a few handfuls of watercress or winter salad leaves

75g walnuts

a handful of fresh mint leaves

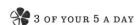 3 OF YOUR 5 A DAY

Place the pomegranates on a hard surface. Use the palm and heel of your hand to firmly roll them back and forth to loosen up the seeds inside.

Set a fine sieve over a bowl. Halve the pomegranates over the sieve, catching the juice. Squeeze the seeds and remaining juice from the fruits. Sift through the seeds and remove any papery yellow bits. Segment the oranges over the pomegranate seeds – you'll use the juice in the bowl to glaze your pigeon breasts.

Rub the garlic into the pigeon breasts. Season well. Place a large frying pan over medium-high heat. Add a splash of olive oil and the rosemary sprig. When hot, add the pigeon. Cook for 3 minutes or until golden on each side.

Remove the pigeon and the rosemary from the pan. Add the orange and pomegranate juice collected in the bowl. Let it boil until it has reduced down to a sticky glaze, it will take a couple of minutes. Remove from the heat when it's as sticky as honey. Place the pigeon in the pan and coat in the sweet glaze. Remove. Scatter the walnuts into the pan and fold through to mop up any remaining syrup.

Arrange the salad leaves on the plates. Top with the orange segments and pomegranate seeds. Thinly slice the pigeon breasts. Lay them over the top. Finish each salad with the walnuts and mint leaves.

Drunken birds on sherry parsnips,
with watercress, pear and hazelnut salad

Pheasant and partridge are quick and easy to cook. They're a great autumnal and winter alternative to chicken and duck, and faster to cook.

SERVES 4

olive oil

2 partridges or pheasants

sea salt and pepper

200ml sherry

4 tablespoons honey

1kg parsnips, peeled and cut into 6cm batons

2 sprigs of rosemary, leaves finely chopped

a few handfuls of watercress

2 ripe pears, peeled and sliced

splash of balsamic vinegar

a handful of hazelnuts, toasted and roughly chopped

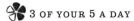 3 OF YOUR 5 A DAY

Preheat the oven to 200°C/gas mark 6.

Heat a frying pan until hot. Add a good splash of olive oil.

Place the parsnips in the pan. Sauté until they start to pick up colour. Splash in 150ml of the sherry. Let it sizzle up, and turn the parsnips to coat. Tumble into a roasting dish. Fold in the chopped rosemary and honey. Season. Pop in the oven for 30 minutes, until nicely caramelised. Meanwhile, season the game birds thoroughly inside and out with salt and pepper.

Place the frying pan back on the heat. Brown the birds all over. Perch them on top of the roasting parsnips. Splash the remaining sherry and any juices from the frying pan over the top of the birds. Cook for 15 minutes.

Remove from the oven. Place the birds on a cutting board to rest. If the parsnips have yet to crisp up and properly colour, give them a little sizzle in the frying pan until they're sticky and golden.

Mix the watercress and pears. Season. Dress with balsamic vinegar and a splash of olive oil. Divide the parsnips between the plates. Carve off a breast and a leg of partridge for each person. Add a mound of salad next to it. Dust a few hazelnuts over the plate and serve.

QUICK GAME STOCK

Don't throw away those partridge bones – they make a wonderful stock, which can be used as a base for a simple root vegetable soup.

TO MAKE First, pluck off any little bits of meat that may still be clinging to the bones. Keep this for the soup below.

Place a pot over medium heat. Add a splash of olive oil. Add the bones, any leftover skin, 1 quartered onion, 2 roughly chopped carrots, a few peppercorns and a handful of thyme or parsley. Fry for a moment, then add just enough water to cover. Bring to the boil, then reduce the heat and simmer for 30 minutes to 1 hour.

Drain, pressing as much water out of the veg as possible. Pour into pots and store in the fridge for up to 3 days, or in the freezer for up to 6 months.

Easy partridge and root soup

Dice whatever root vegetables you have to hand: carrots, parsnips, swede, turnips, celeriac, Jerusalem artichokes...

Fry with 1 finely chopped onion and 2 chopped garlic cloves. Add 2–3 rashers of diced bacon, if you like. Sauté until the vegetables are soft and starting to pick up a bit of colour. Get the bacon nicely coloured, if you're using it, too.

Sprinkle in a few herbs, such as thyme leaves or chopped rosemary. Add a splash of sherry, port or wine. Let it bubble up.

Pour in the stock and any leftover partridge meat. Crumble in some cooked chestnuts, if you like. You can also stir in some finely chopped cabbage or kale. Or do both.

Let it warm through and serve with a big wedge of bread brushed with olive oil, or scatter torn hunks of fried bread over the top. Simple and delicious.

Venison fajitas

Venison steaks are meltingly tender and work beautifully in fajitas. The meat is great, too, because it doesn't need very long to cook, making it ideal for this flash-in-the-pan meal.

SERVES 4 GENEROUSLY

1 venison steak

2 garlic cloves, finely minced

a splash of olive oil

sea salt and black pepper

½ teaspoon ground cumin

½ teaspoon paprika

2 red onions, finely sliced

2 red, yellow or orange peppers, deseeded and sliced

8 flour tortilla wraps

2 avocados, sliced just before serving

2 tomatoes, diced

2 limes or 1 lemon

a handful of fresh coriander leaves

🍀 2.5–3 OF YOUR 5 A DAY

Place the venison in a bowl. Massage the garlic and a bit of olive oil into the steak. Dust with a good pinch of salt and pepper. Add the cumin and paprika. Rub it in nicely.

Place a large frying pan over medium-high heat. Add a little splash of olive oil. When it's hot, place the steak in the pan and cook, untouched, for 1 minute. Give the pan a shake. Cook for 3 minutes more. Flip and cook for 5 minutes on that side. This will give you a medium-rare steak. Add 2 minutes to the cooking time for medium, and 4 for well-done.

Once the steak is cooked, remove from the pan and set aside.

Add a bit more oil to the pan and fry the onions and peppers until nicely softened and deliciously aromatic.

Warm the tortillas in a dry, clean frying pan until just softened. Pile the onions and peppers into the centre of each tortilla.

Thinly slice the venison steak. Top each tortilla with a few slivers. Top with avocado slices, diced tomato, a good squeeze of lemon or lime juice and a handful of fresh coriander leaves. Serve.

MORE WAYS WITH VENISON

Venison can be treated in much the same way as beef. So, if you bought two venison steaks (they normally come in a pack of two), try it instead of beef in one of the following recipes. It works beautifully.

Simple beef curry PAGE 32

Ranch-hand steak salad PAGE 38

Mushroom burgers with apple beetroot slaw PAGE 42

FISH

If the world remains on its current path of overfishing, by 2050 all fish stocks could be uneconomical to exploit or actually extinct.

The key here is to not fixate on a single fish that appears on the sustainable charts because overindulging in it could quickly make the species threatened. This is why I'm not going to offer a guide of 'Fish to Eat' and 'Fish not to Eat'. The best advice is to give your diet as much breadth and variety as possible. There are lots of different fish in the sea that most of us have yet to discover. Seeking them makes eating more exciting. It also offers your body greater access to different nutrients. Use the buying guide opposite to help navigate your way around the fish counter.

There are a few fish, however, that I would suggest you avoid: salmon and tuna. These species are highly overfished. These big fish also need to eat lots of little fish in order to thrive.

It can take up to 20kg of wild fish, such as anchovies, sardines and mackerel, to produce 1kg of ranched tuna.

Demand for salmon is so intense that there are plans for it to be genetically modified. There's a similar, if not a stronger, worry with tuna. It's the most consumed fish in the world. As a result, some tuna species are on the brink of collapse – in other words, our children's children may never get to taste tuna.

Most of us have probably had a lifetime's supply of both anyway. As there are so many other sustainable fish out there to try, it's well worth moving on from overfished salmon and tuna in favour of something new, exciting and all-round healthier.

One of the easiest ways to land a catch of healthy, sustainable fish is to find a trustworthy fishmonger. They should be able to tell you exactly where and how your fish was caught. If they can't tell you this information, find a new person to buy your fish from – the good ones (there are plenty out there) really know their stuff. Simply tell them that you're looking to buy sustainable fish. Their eyes normally light up. Fishmongers love being asked questions and they want to see people moving toward better fish choices. Fish are their livelihood, after all.

FISH BUYING GUIDE

Below are key things to look out and ask for when buying fish. Stick with the same criteria when ordering fish at restaurants.

SEEK

Locally caught fish from fisherman who go out on small boats for hours, not days, at a time.

Seafood from fishermen who limit the number of fish they catch.

Fish caught from plentiful stocks.

Mature fish caught outside their spawning season; this means they have had a chance to reproduce and replenish stocks.

Sustainable fishing methods: line-caught; dive-caught; hand gathered; hand-line; jig, pot or creel; rod and line.

AVOID

Small fish such as whitebait (normally baby herring) which have yet to reach maturity and reproduce.

Buying fish during its spawning season which is when they're trying to reproduce; this keeps the fish stocks healthy.

Fish caught by longlines, trawling, dredging or purse seines.

Fish caught from large boats that spend weeks at sea.

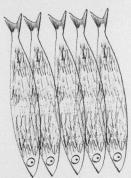

WHERE TO BUY YOUR FISH

If you can't find a good fishmonger or a farmers' market with a good fish supplier, seek out a Community Supported Fisheries scheme – or start one up yourself. This is similar to Community Supported Agriculture, whereby you pay a subscription to a farmer/fisherman as you would for a magazine, but instead of a magazine each month, you get locally grown food/caught fish in return for your investment.

The idea behind such schemes is sustainability so your money not only buys you amazing, healthy food, it also supports the local community and environment.

Fish tacos with beach bum salsa

The light golden batter encasing these little nuggets of fish is based on one from a fish and chips shop in Yorkshire, England. They use cold water in the batter, instead of beer, which really lets the fish shine through.

SERVES 4

BEACH BUM SALSA

1 red pepper, deseeded and finely diced

1 small pineapple, peeled and finely diced

6 spring onions, finely sliced

juice and zest of 1 lime

1 teaspoon white wine vinegar

1 teaspoon caster sugar

2 teaspoons olive oil

½ chilli, deseeded, minced

small handful of fresh coriander, finely chopped

BATTER AND FISH

110g self-raising flour

½ teaspoon sea salt

pinch of cayenne pepper

juice and zest of 1 lemon

few sprigs of fresh coriander, finely chopped

200g sustainable white fish, such as pollack

250ml sunflower oil

TO SERVE

8 flour tortilla wraps

crisp lettuce leaves

2 ripe avocados, peeled and thinly sliced

coriander leaves and lime wedges

🍀 2.5 OF YOUR 5 A DAY

For the salsa, combine all the ingredients in a large bowl. Salsa can be prepared one day ahead — if you are making it in advance, wait to add the coriander until right before serving. Cover and refrigerate.

For the fish, pour the oil into a large pot and place over medium heat. Make up the batter by sifting the flour, salt and cayenne into a bowl. Fold in the coriander. Make a well in the centre. Add the lemon juice and 125ml cold water and whisk until smooth.

Cut the fish into 3cm hunks. Dip them into the batter and thoroughly coat. When the oil is hot (test by adding a dot of batter, if it sizzles and firms up immediately, it's ready), carefully add the fish in small batches. Fry until crisp and golden, 3–5 minutes.

Drain the fish on paper or a few slices of stale bread to soak up excess oil. Dust with a good sprinkle of sea salt while the fish is still hot.

Before serving, brush each tortilla with olive oil and warm each for 30 seconds (oil-side down) in a hot pan. Wrap the tortillas in a clean cloth to keep them warm.

Assemble the tacos any way you fancy, but a great way of layering textures and flavours is to open up the warm tortillas, lay a lettuce leaf or two in the centre of each, top with avocado slices, a spoonful of salsa and pile the fish on top. Finish with coriander leaves and an extra squeeze of lime. Wrap up and tuck in.

Tandoori-spiced black bream with watermelon salad

*You can use this elegant tandoori spice blend on just about everything,
including meat and vegetables. I've chosen it as a rub for black bream because
it's a firm, meaty (as well as sustainable) fish. It is ideal grilled whole, so you
can rub the spice on the skin, forming a delicious earthy crust.*

SERVES 4

1 large or 2 small whole black bream

olive oil

FOR THE TANDOORI SPICE BLEND

3 tablespoons paprika

1 tablespoon each ground coriander, ground cumin and sea salt

1¼ teaspoons each freshly ground black pepper, sugar and ground ginger

½ teaspoon each ground cinnamon and crumbled saffron threads

¼ teaspoon cayenne pepper

FOR THE WATERMELON SALAD

1 tablespoon olive oil

½ teaspoon finely grated fresh ginger

juice and zest of 1 lime

1 mini watermelon or ½ medium-sized melon, cut into bite-sized cubes

2 handfuls watercress, thick stems trimmed

½ cucumber, peeled and cubed

3 spring onions, thinly sliced

a handful of fresh mint leaves, roughly chopped

 2 OF YOUR 5 A DAY

Preheat the oven to 200°C/gas mark 6.

Mix all the spices together. Rinse the fish and pat dry. Cut three 1cm deep slits at a diagonal across each side of the fish. This will help the bream cook faster, and get more flavour into the fish.

Rub the olive oil over the fish. Give each side a good dusting of the spice blend, rubbing it into the skin and inside the slits you've cut. Place on an oiled roasting tray or grill pan and cook for 7–10 minutes on each side, or until the fish easily flakes and is white right down to the bone.

To make the salad, place the oil, ginger, lime juice and zest in a large bowl. Add the watermelon and all the remaining ingredients to the bowl and toss to coat. Divide the salad among four plates and serve.

Carve hunks off the fish and serve alongside the Watermelon Salad.

TIP If you have a cupboard full of neglected spices, like me, this is a great way to shift them. Store the remaining spice mix in an airtight jar — it will keep for ages. It's perfect for kebabs – see the Barbecue section on page 62 for ideas – or slather it on the Roast Leg of Lamb (pages 50-51) in place of rosemary and garlic.

Simple sand sole
with lemon, avocado and butter bean salad

This is one of the fastest ways to cook fish, and you can pretty much apply it to any fish you like. Just lightly dust the fish with seasoned flour and pan fry in olive oil. That's it. The salad is elegant, yet substantial, which means that you only need a small serving of fish alongside it.

SERVES 4

400g tinned butter beans, drained and rinsed

400g cherry tomatoes, halved

sea salt and black pepper

2 avocados, halved and de-stoned

2 lemons

a pinch of chilli powder (optional)

a handful of fresh basil, leaves torn

olive oil

4 sand sole fillets, or any other sustainable flat fish

plain white flour, for dusting the fish

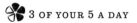 3 OF YOUR 5 A DAY

First make the salad by simply mixing the beans and tomatoes. Season.

Cut each avocado half into three pieces. Peel back the skin and add these chunky slices to the beans and tomatoes.

Add the juice and zest of the lemons, then add a pinch of chilli powder (if using), the basil and a good glug of olive oil. Set aside.

Place a large frying pan over medium-high heat. Season the fish and generously dust with flour. Shake off any excess. Add a splash of olive oil to the frying pan. Once hot, add the fish and cook for 2–3 minutes, or until golden on each side.

Serve the fish alongside a mound of the salad, along with wedges of the remaining lemon and a crisp white wine.

Thai-spiced fishcakes with som tam salad

Turning fish into fishcakes is a great way to make small amounts go a long way. However, I haven't bulked these little Thai ones out with potato. They're small but they have a good proportion of fish, with only a little dusting of breadcrumbs. With the peanut-topped salad, it's a healthy, well-balanced meal.

SERVES 4

200g sustainable white fish

3 tablespoons Thai green curry paste

4 heaped tablespoons breadcrumbs

a little flour, for dusting

olive oil

sea salt

FOR THE SOM TAM SALAD

2 courgettes, trimmed

3 medium carrots, trimmed

1 firm mango (so not too ripe)

1 garlic clove, chopped

1 small red chilli, deseeded and sliced lengthways

½ teaspoon sea salt

juice and zest of 2 limes

1 teaspoon sugar or 2 teaspoons honey

a handful of fresh coriander leaves

100g roasted peanuts, roughly crushed, to serve

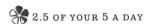 2.5 OF YOUR 5 A DAY

Roughly chop the fish and place it in a food-processor with the curry paste. Pulse until you have a coarse paste — don't whip it up too finely.

If you don't have a food-processor, just lay the fish and curry paste on a large cutting board and chop with a big knife, pressing with the side of the knife to mash and mix the fish with the curry paste.

Fold in the breadcrumbs and shape into balls. Dust with a little flour to keep them from sticking. You should be able to get eight little fish cakes out of the mixture, giving you two for each person. Pop them into the fridge to firm up for 30 minutes.

Meanwhile, make the salad. Using a vegetable peeler, peel the courgettes along their length, then just keep going, making strips of the flesh until you reach the seed pod in the centre. Nibble the seed pod while you cook or thinly slice it and add it to the salad. Peel the carrot in the same way.

Peel one side of the mango using a vegetable peeler and then shave off long, thin slivers of the mango flesh with the peeler, so it's similar in shape and texture to the courgettes and carrots. Continue around the whole of the mango until you've used most of it up. Save any remaining bits of mango for a fruit salad.

Mix the courgettes, carrot and mango together with the garlic, chilli, salt, lime juice and zest, and sugar or honey. Set aside while you fry the fishcakes. Press each ball down into a little cake and fry in olive oil until golden on each side. Serve with the som tam salad and garnish with coriander leaves and crushed peanuts.

Sweet potato crab cakes with pan-roasted salsa

Crab meat is extremely nutritious. Just 50g of brown crab meat provides one-third of your omega 3 for an entire week. You could serve these crab cakes with avocado slices and corn on the cob to make a complete meal.

SERVES 4

2 sweet potatoes (400–500g), peeled and cut into small cubes

75g fine polenta (cornmeal), plus extra for dusting

½ sweet red pepper, deseeded and very finely diced

½ onion, very finely chopped

1 garlic clove, finely chopped

200g cooked brown crab meat

juice and zest of 1 lime, plus a quartered lime for serving

1 teaspoon Tabasco

a good handful of fresh coriander, finely chopped

sea salt and black pepper

olive or sunflower oil for frying

FOR THE PAN-ROASTED SALSA

250g cherry tomatoes

½ onion, halved

2 garlic cloves, peeled but left whole

1 red or green chilli (to taste)

juice of 1 lime

a pinch of caster sugar

sea salt and black pepper

a large handful of coriander leaves, finely chopped

✿ WITH A DAB OF SALSA, 2–3 CRAB CAKES EQUAL 3 OF YOUR 5 A DAY

Boil or steam the sweet potatoes until soft. Drain and mash. While still warm, stir through the polenta. Pop a lid on and let it steam for 10 minutes. This will soften the polenta and thicken the mixture.

Fold the remaining ingredients through, taste, and season if needed. Form into 8 large or 12 smaller crab cakes. Lightly coat each cake with a little polenta if they're looking a bit soft or wet.

To make the salsa, place a frying pan over medium-high heat. Put the tomatoes, onion, garlic and chilli in the pan and dry-roast for 10–15 minutes, turning the vegetables a few times until they start to pick up colour.

Place the warm veg in a blender or food-processor with the lime juice and a pinch of sugar. Pulse until chopped. Taste and season as needed. If the salsa's looking a bit too wet, place it back in the warm roasting pan to thicken it up. Set aside.

Shallow fry the crab cakes in a good splash of oil. Finish with a sprinkling of salt and a squeeze of lime. Scatter the coriander leaves over the salsa and serve it alongside the crab cakes.

Lemon herb fish cakes

These are your classic fishcakes, which contain a good bit of potato. They're a great way of getting fish into fish-sceptical children (and adults). But, if you want to up the fish flavour, use oily fish such as sardines or mackerel to make them.

SERVES 4

200g sustainable white or oily fish

500g mashed potato

juice and zest of 1 lemon, plus lemon wedges to serve

2 teaspoons Dijon mustard

2 tablespoons capers

a large handful of tarragon, basil, chives and/or parsley

a pinch of chilli powder (optional)

sea salt and black pepper

2.5 OF YOUR 5 A DAY WHEN SERVED WITH BROCCOLI, CARROTS AND PEAS

Place the fish in a frying pan. Cover with water and poach for 2–3 minutes on each side, until the fish is tender and flakes easily with a fork. Remove from the pan.

Mix the fish with the potatoes, lemon juice and zest, mustard, capers and herbs. Season well. Once everything is nicely mixed, shape into 8 round patties.

Fry each fish cake in olive oil until golden on each side. Serve with lemon wedges and a medley of steamed broccoli, carrots and peas.

Mussels in a red dress

If you've never cooked mussels before, this is a good dish to launch your mussel-cooking career. It's extremely easy and should take no longer than 30 minutes start to finish.

As further bait to tempt you: mussels rank high in the sustainability charts, even farmed ones. To encourage mussels to grow, fishermen lay down a series of ropes to which the mussels attach themselves. These ropes attract all kinds of seaweeds which act almost like an underwater rainforest. This is great for biodiversity.

SERVES 4

1kg rope-grown mussels, cleaned (see note below)

a splash of olive oil

5 garlic cloves, finely chopped

½ teaspoon dried red chilli or a sliver of fresh red chilli, finely chopped

400g tinned tomatoes

400g fresh tomatoes, diced

2 tablespoons tomato paste

1½ tablespoons capers

5 tablespoons Kalamata olives, pitted and chopped

100ml red wine

400g linguine, spaghetti or tagliatelle

a handful of fresh basil, finely chopped

 2 OF YOUR 5 A DAY

Just before cooking, clean the mussels by scrubbing them well with a brush under cold water and scraping off any barnacles with a knife. If the beard is still attached, remove it by pulling it from tip to hinge or by pulling and cutting it off with a knife.

Warm a large frying pan over medium-high heat. Add a splash of olive oil. Stir the garlic and chilli through the warm oil, until fragrant but not browned, about 2 minutes.

Add the tomatoes, tomato paste, capers, olives and wine. Simmer, uncovered, stirring occasionally and breaking up the tomatoes, until the sauce is thick, 20–25 minutes.

Cook the pasta until al dente. Drain and drizzle with olive oil.

While the pasta cooks, fill a large pot with just enough water to cover the base (a depth of about 2cm) and place over medium heat. Add the mussels, then cook, covered, until they just open wide, checking frequently after 3 minutes. Transfer to a bowl. (Discard any mussels that remain unopened after 6 minutes.)

Add the basil to the sauce and fold through the pasta. Divide between 4 plates and pile a handful of mussels on top of each serving.

NOTE The quantity of mussels looks quite generous here because I'm counting the meat inside the shells and not the weight of the shells. As a general rule, the meat to shell ratio is one-third. So, 1kg of mussels offers you only about 330g meat.

I've also accounted for shells that are opened (which you should discard) prior to cooking, and ones that are still shut after cooking (which you should also throw out).

Crab tagliatelle with chilli, cherry tomatoes and broccoli

This recipe is inspired by Richard Corner. He and his fisherman brother Neville have a crab company, Seafood and Eat It, in Newlyn, Cornwall. The crab they source is caught using pots. This is the preferred method. Richard explains: 'Traditional pots do not damage the seabed, and anything other than crabs is able to escape. Furthermore, fisherman hand -check the crabs and throw back any carrying eggs, and those that are too small.'

SERVES 4

400g tagliatelle

300g purple sprouting broccoli, tenderstem or regular broccoli florets

4 garlic cloves, peeled and finely chopped

500g fresh cherry tomatoes, halved or quartered

2 fresh red chillies, deseeded and finely chopped (to taste)

200g fresh, cooked white crab meat (or a mix of brown and white)

zest and juice of 2 lemons

sea salt

a large handful of fresh basil leaves, roughly chopped

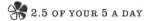 2.5 OF YOUR 5 A DAY

Cook the pasta. Just before it's done, add the broccoli to the pot. Put the lid on and steam for a moment. Drain. Drizzle with olive oil and add a pinch of salt. Set aside.

Sauté the garlic and tomatoes in a splash of olive oil for a minute or two. Toss in the red chilli, cooked tagliatelle and broccoli, crab, lemon juice and zest. Keep it in the pan, over the heat, just long enough to let the crab warm through. Season.

Pile on to plates and top with basil leaves and a finishing touch of olive oil. Serve warm.

SOURCING AND COOKING CRAB

The best crab meat comes from crabs that have been cooked moments after they've left the sea. I don't live near the sea, so I tend to buy my fresh crab from a fishmonger or a farmers' market, as they can deliver crab that has been freshly cooked and I don't have to worry about transporting a live crab home. This is a great way of having fresh crab without the hassle.

If you want to cook your own crab, the most humane method is to place the crab in the freezer for an hour. This should ensure that the crabs are rendered completely unconscious by the time they are plunged into boiling water.

Use about 100g of salt to every litre of water, and use enough water to fully cover the crab. Weigh the crab. Then calculate the cooking time: you'll need to simmer for 15 minutes for the first 500g, and add a further 10 minutes for every extra 500g. You will know when your crab is cooked, as its shell will turn either pink or brown.

Crab salad with mango, chilli and lime

Another notch in the belt for crab's sustainability is that they're reproducers.
A single crab can have up to 5 million babies.

SERVES 4

2 ripe mangos

2 ripe avocados

1 cucumber

200g Thai rice noodles

4 tablespoons rice vinegar
or verjuice

2 red chillies, deseeded and
finely chopped (more or less,
to taste)

200g fresh crab meat
(preferably a mix of brown and
white but one or the other is
fine)

juice and zest of 2 limes

a large handful of fresh
coriander, basil and/or mint
leaves

sea salt and black pepper

a few handfuls of baby
salad leaves

olive oil

2 tablespoons coconut chips,
toasted

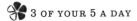 3 OF YOUR 5 A DAY

Cut the mango, avocado and cucumber into 1cm dice. Add a splash of the lime juice and a pinch of salt. Toss and set aside.

Cook the noodles according to the instructions on the pack — they should only need 3 minutes in boiling water. Drain, rinse with cool water and then toss into a bowl with the rice vinegar or verjuice. Add the chilli, crab and remaining lime juice. Season.

Arrange the salad leaves on plates. Combine the cubed mango salad with the leaves. Place the crab noodles in the centre and top with the toasted coconut and the herbs. Serve immediately.

Fish stock

It may sound daunting but fish stock is one of the easiest stocks you can make, especially as it requires minimal cooking. It's delicious as a base for the Fishmonger's Soup (see opposite) or a fennel risotto.

MAKES A 500G POT

bones and heads from 1–2 fish and/or a few handfuls shellfish shells (see note)

olive oil

1 leek, washed and roughly chopped

1 large onion or 3 shallots, roughly chopped

1 fennel, roughly chopped

125ml dry white wine or cider

750ml water

a few peppercorns

1 bay leaf, or a handful of parsley or tarragon

Wash the fish bones in cold water. Remove any traces of blood — don't be squeamish, just rinse under water and they should go.

Add a splash of oil to a wide-bottomed pot. Add the vegetables and sauté for a few minutes.

Add the bones. Turn them over in the oil to cook for a few minutes – this will draw out some of their flavour and goodness. After a minute or two, pour in the wine or cider. Let it reduce down a bit.

Add the water, peppercorns and herbs and bring to a gentle boil. Simmer for 20 minutes.

Remove from the heat and let the stock sit for 10 minutes. Strain into pots and store in the fridge for up to 24 hours, or in the freezer for up to 3 months.

NOTE The only bones that don't work for making stock are those from oily fish such as mackerel and sardines because they are too strongly flavoured. Best bones (and fish heads) to use include those from turbot, sole, gurnard, hake, bass, mullet and whiting. You can also use any skin or fish trimmings that remain if you have filleted your own fish. Good shells to use in fish stock are those from lobster, crab and langoustine.

Fishmonger's soup

Let your fishmonger inspire the star of this soup. Going to them with a recipe to hand is a great way to get the conversation going. Wander in and tell them that you're going to make a classic saffron-kissed tomato and fennel fish soup. Let them recommend a great, sustainable catch from there. They can also fillet and remove any small bones for you.

SERVES 4

500ml fish stock (or use chicken or veg stock)

250g new potatoes, cut into bite-sized hunks

2 white onions, finely chopped

1 carrot, finely diced

2 sticks celery, finely diced

2 garlic cloves, finely chopped

1 fennel bulb, finely diced

a splash of olive oil

250ml white wine

800g tinned tomatoes

1 bay leaf (optional)

1 gurnard, red snapper or any sustainable fish or shellfish (200–300g), boned and cut into chunks

a generous pinch of saffron

juice and zest of 1 lemon

a large handful of fresh tarragon, leaves roughly chopped

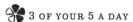 3 OF YOUR 5 A DAY

Place the stock in a saucepan. Add the potatoes and gently boil for 20–30 minutes, or until tender.

While they cook away, sweat the onions, carrot, celery, garlic and fennel in a little olive oil until softened but not coloured, 10–15 minutes.

Add the wine and reduce by half. Add the plum tomatoes, fish stock, potatoes and bay leaf (if using). Simmer for 20 minutes.

Add your fish, along with the saffron and lemon juice and zest. Simmer for 3–5 minutes, until the fish cooks through. Add the tarragon and serve with a delicious loaf of sourdough bread.

NOTE If you don't fancy filleting your own fish, get your fishmonger to do it for you. A good fish shop will also sell its own homemade stock. Get a pot of this for the soup, or make your own (see recipe opposite). If they've filleted your fish for you, they can package up the bones and head needed for the stock separately.

Pack the hamper, we're going on a picnic

If you fill your plate full and try everything, you'll clock up your entire 5 A Day with this Italian-inspired picnic spread. It's perfect for a summer weekend lunch.

Blueberry lemonade

Whizzing blueberries into your lemonade sweetens it, transforms it to a stunning deep purplish hue and also gives a generous nudge towards your daily fruit intake.

SERVES 6

150ml freshly squeezed lemon juice, about 5 lemons' worth, plus lemon slices to garnish

200ml water

200g blueberries

75g caster sugar

 0.5 OF YOUR 5 A DAY

Place all the ingredients in a blender and whizz to a smooth purée. Strain into a jug over ice. If you like, add a few fresh blueberries and lemon slices to garnish.

TIP: make this a day or so in advance and freeze the lemonade in ice-cube trays. Pop the ice cubes in a jug and let them melt as you venture to your picnic spot. You should end up with an icy, slushy, deliciously refreshing lemonade.

Pat-in-the-pan olive oil pastry

This pastry is quick and easy because you don't have to mess around with rolling it out. It saves your countertop from a floury mess and is a great one for those less experienced with pastry-making. Using olive oil instead of butter makes it lighter.

MAKES ENOUGH FOR THE SPINACH TART BELOW OR WHOLESOME CHICKEN PIE (PAGE 107)

150g plain white, stoneground flour

¼ teaspoon sea salt

75ml olive oil

2–3 tablespoons cold water

Preheat the oven to 230°C/gas mark 8.

Mix the flour and salt. Add the oil and fold through until all the flour is moistened. Sprinkle with the cold water, 1 tablespoon at a time, tossing with a fork until all the water is absorbed. Gather the pastry into a ball. Divide it into smaller balls if you're making individual tarts.

Plonk the ball or balls down into the middle of your tart pan or pans. Press into the bottom and up the sides of the dish. Try to smooth it over to make the crust even. Prick the bottom and sides of the pastry thoroughly with a fork. Bake blind for 10–12 minutes or until light brown. Cool before adding your filling.

Creamy spinach tart

Tarts make a wonderful centrepiece for a picnic. To keep the custard base of the tart dense, it's richer with egg yolks than whites. Use the spare whites to make the macaroons on page 163.

SERVES 6

olive oil

2 garlic cloves, finely chopped

250g spinach

sea salt and black pepper

Pat-in-the-Pan Olive Oil Pastry, see above

1 whole egg and 2 egg yolks

100ml double cream

2 teaspoons Dijon mustard

50g Parmesan cheese, freshly grated

❁ 0.5 OF YOUR 5 A DAY

Place a lidded pot big enough for the spinach over medium heat. Add a splash of oil and sauté the garlic until soft, then add the spinach. Season. Cook until the spinach is just wilted, about 7 minutes. Place in a colander and carefully press out the bitter juices.

Bake your pastry crust blind, if you haven't already, according to the instructions above. Reduce the oven heat to 180°C/gas mark 4.

Whisk the eggs, cream and mustard until smooth. Fold in the Parmesan. Season. Swirl the spinach through the cream mixture. Pour over the base of the tart.

Bake in the oven for 25–30 minutes, or until just golden and set.

Cool for at least 10 minutes before cutting. Refrigerate for up to 3 days.

Zesty potato salad

I'm not a big fan of store-bought mayonnaise – it contains far too much gunk and I'm usually too lazy to make my own. So, I wanted to come up with a delicious potato salad that was mayo-free. This has become a picnic favourite.

SERVES 6

1kg new potatoes

8 spring onions, finely sliced

sea salt and black pepper

4 tablespoons Dijon mustard

100ml olive oil

juice and zest of 1 orange

2 tablespoons cider or white wine vinegar

a generous handful of herbs (such as parsley, mint, chives and/or basil), roughly chopped

 0.25 OF YOUR 5 A DAY

Halve or quarter the potatoes and lightly boil them until tender. Toss them in a large bowl with the spring onions. Season and set aside.

Whisk the mustard, oil, orange juice and zest and vinegar to make the salad dressing.

Once the potatoes cool, mix them in the bowl with the dressing. Fold in the herbs and store in the fridge until ready to serve.

Tuscan stale bread salad

A classic Italian salad, loaded with veg. Perfect with the tart and potato salad.

SERVES 6

3 red or yellow peppers

4–5 slices stale rustic bread

3 tablespoons olive oil, plus extra for oiling

750g tomatoes, diced

1 garlic clove, finely chopped

3 spring onions, sliced

100g pitted olives

a large handful of fresh basil, roughly chopped

3 tablespoons white wine vinegar

sea salt and black pepper

 2.5 OF YOUR 5 A DAY

Preheat the oven to 200°C/gas mark 6.

Cut the peppers into 2cm hunks and tear the bread into 1cm cubes. Place on a well-oiled baking tray and mix through the oil. Roast for 15 minutes until the peppers are soft and the croutons golden.

Place the tomatoes, garlic, spring onions and olives in a large bowl. Dress with the olive oil, vinegar, black pepper and a touch of salt. Mix everything together. Add the peppers and toasted bread when they're ready.

Top with the basil and pack up the salad until ready to serve. It will keep for 24 hours.

Macaroons with vanilla strawberries and nectarines

These almondy macaroons are a cross between the delicate French patisserie ones and the more robust and chewy Italian rendition. They're a delicious way to use up the egg whites leftover from making Creamy Spinach Tart (page 159).

MAKES 12

100g ground almonds

150g golden icing sugar

2 tablespoons cornflour

½ vanilla pod, seeds scraped and pod saved for fruit

2 egg whites

5–6 tablespoons strawberry or raspberry jam

grated zest of 1 lemon

400g strawberries

4 ripe nectarines, halved

 **WITH THE FRUIT, YOU GET 2 OF YOUR 5 A DAY**

Preheat the oven to 160°C/gas mark 3.

Mix the ground almonds, icing sugar, lemon zest and vanilla together.

In a separate large bowl, whisk the egg whites until they form soft peaks. Take a large metal spoon and gently fold a third of the sugary almond mixture into the egg whites until smooth. Repeat until all the almonds are incorporated into the mixture.

Carefully drop the mixture by the teaspoon on to a good non-stick or a greaseproof paper-lined baking sheet – leave 3cm between each spoonful and make sure the spoonfuls are even-sized. Prepare two baking sheets if you can; if not, you'll have to bake these in batches.

Bake for 12–15 minutes, or until firm, glossy on top and just golden. Use a thin spatula or fish slice to gently lift the cooked macaroons from the tray while they're still warm.

Sandwich the macaroons together, using about 1 teaspoon of jam per pair. Store in an airtight container for up to 24 hours. Serve with the fruit salad below.

For the fruit salad: place the strawberries (trim the tops if you like) and halved nectarines in a separate container. Add the empty vanilla pod. Fold it through so that its flavour can mingle with the fruit. Refrigerate until ready to serve.

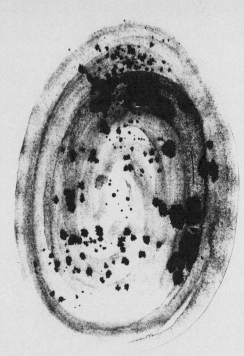

EGGS

Eggs are nature's perfect food, especially when you buy them from truly free-range, outdoor-reared hens. One egg from an outdoor chicken can give you more than 60 per cent of your daily recommended dose of vitamin D. Hens penned up in cages have no access to omega-rich grasses, vitamin D-giving sunshine and fat-lowering exercise, whereas free-range hens have an abundance of this goodness which gets packed into every egg they lay.

Just one egg from a healthy, happy, free-range bird will give you so much more than several cheaper eggs from a caged hen.

When you go for this healthier option, you're also benefiting the environment. The consequences of intensively laid eggs are severe. As with chickens reared for meat, egg-laying hens that are not eating grass are often fed pellets made from soya and a lot of this soya is grown on cleared rainforests. It's shipped around the world and it's highly processed.

It also makes for pretty dull-tasting eggs. In Nicolette Hahn Niman's book *Righteous Porkchop: Finding a Life and Good Food Beyond Factory Farms,* she outlines her quest to source traditionally-reared eggs – ones from a small farm, rather than a large-scale, factory-like operation. 'I located yet another person in town with a poultry flock that ranges in pasture and eats only natural feeds. She keeps five or six chicken breeds, each

From outdoor, free-range, hens you get:

- *Four to six times more vitamin D*
- *Two-thirds more vitamin A*
- *Up to ten times more omega 3*
- *Three times more vitamin E*
- *Seven times more beta carotene*
- *One third less cholesterol*
- *One quarter less saturated fat*
- *Ten per cent less overall fat*
- *A better-tasting egg*

providing a distinctly different egg. In colour, the eggs are everything from pale blue and green to a flecked dark terracotta and deep tan.

'I look forward to opening a carton of these eggs almost as much as a box of chocolates... the greatest reward is in the eating. The yolks are dense and deep golden, like a ripe persimmon. The colour's intensity comes from the xanthophylls of the plants on which the hens munch. The mass-produced variety – even if they're 'organic' – simply cannot hold a candle to the richness, flavour and beauty of these eggs.'

This extract makes me hungry every time I read it. So, where do you find delicious eggs like the one Nicolette describes? There are many options, including small farmshops and delis; home delivery companies and farmers' markets; and some farms have box schemes which allow you to order eggs and plenty of other things to your door direct. Even some supermarkets now sell pretty good eggs.

If you have the space, you could even raise your own hens. There are some great books and courses to get you started. In many places, there are now charities that will help you adopt (usually for free) an ex-battery hen.

As well as sourcing top-notch eggs for your breakfast or dinner, look into the origin of the eggs in the food you buy, such as cakes, biscuits, mayonnaise; eggs are even used to make wine (egg whites are sometimes used to purify wine, which is fine if it's come from a good source).

Put pressure on producers of these foods to source the right eggs. Hellmann's mayonnaise responded to demand and vowed to source only free-range eggs for its UK-made products. Get the producers of your favourite egg-containing products to do the same. Your voice can be a powerful tool in turning the food system back in the right direction.

Hens in intensive systems are killed after a year, but happy, lazy free-range hens can live from five to 10 years.

Things to look out for when buying eggs:
- *The name of the farm; even better: the name of the farmer.*
- *The breed of hen laying the egg – heritage breeds are top notch.*

HOW TO BOIL AN EGG

The world's top chefs cannot even agree on this one. I once conducted a survey – asking a few Michelin-starred and celebrity chefs for their tips and this is the method that came out on top:

Bring your egg to room temperature (i.e. take out of the fridge the night before, or at least 30 minutes before cooking).

If you're not organised enough to take your egg out the night before (like me), run it under warm water before boiling. In this case, you'll need to add 1 extra minute to the boiling times given below.

Bring a small pot of water to the boil; ensure the water is deep enough to fully cover the egg.

Place the egg in the boiling water – make sure it's not boiling too vigorously as it will toss the egg around and crack it.

Set a timer for 5 minutes. Let the water bubble away gently. Remove the egg as soon as the timer goes off. This will give you a soft-boiled egg. Cook 1 minute longer for a yolk that's a little less runny.

Duck eggs take 7 minutes to cook, if you want them soft boiled.

Boiled egg and a selection of soldiers

Did you hear about the French chef who made his omelettes with only one egg? 'After all', he said, 'One egg is un oeuf!'... Tish, boom.

Well, with a decent section of dippers, one egg can make a wholesome, nourishing meal. Try this with a duck egg; they're a bit bigger, have a wider girth and a richer yolk.

SERVES 1

1 egg

2-3 toast fingers, brushed with a fruity olive oil

a little pot of good sea salt

✿ 2.5 OF YOUR 5 A DAY

Simply serve your freshly boiled egg (see boiling tips, above) with a selection of dippers. You need three of the suggested veg dippers below to get your 2.5 servings in.

DIPPERS

2-3 asparagus spears, lightly steamed
2-3 sprouting broccoli spears, lightly steamed
2-3 slender carrots, steamed until tender
2-3 breakfast radishes
2-3 slender sticks of celery

Baker's egg with breakfast salad

This is a famous dish at the Mill Bakery in Lyme Regis, Dorset. It consists of a thick slice of fresh organic bread that's had a hole cut out of the centre and an egg dropped into it. It's baked until the egg has just set, which gives the bread a golden-toasty crunch on top, while leaving it soft on the bottom.

It's a weekend favourite in my house. We always have it with a salad made with seasonal fruit and leaves. It balances the plate and means you're satisfied with just one egg.

FOR EACH PERSON, YOU NEED

1 doorstopper-sized slice of bread from a good loaf (sourdough works beautifully)

1 egg

olive oil

sea salt

FOR THE BREAKFAST SALAD, PER PERSON

a handful of baby salad, rocket or watercress leaves

some fresh mint or basil

a handful fresh or dried fruit (such as strawberries, grapes, figs, pear, melon, peaches, dried apricots...)

a drizzle of honey

a splash of balsamic vinegar

a drop of olive or almond oil

a sprinkling of toasted nuts

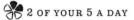 2 OF YOUR 5 A DAY

Preheat the oven to 180°C/gas mark 4. Brush your bread with olive oil all over – sides and crust. Cut a hole out of the centre of the bread using a round biscuit cutter or the rim of a decent-sized cup.

Place the holey bread on an oiled baking tray. Break the egg into the centre. Place the cut-out circle of bread on the tray next to the large slice.

Sprinkle a pinch of salt over the egg and bread. Bake for 7–10 minutes, or until the egg is set to your liking.

To make the Breakfast salad, scatter the leaves on a plate with the herbs. Tumble the fruit on top and gently mix it through the leaves. Drizzle the honey over. Splash over a few drops of balsamic vinegar and a little drizzle of olive oil. Top with almonds and serve.

Asparagus frittata

Frittatas are great carriers for seasonal vegetables when there's some melted cheese thrown into the equation. Asparagus, mushrooms and Taleggio is my favourite combo in springtime. Do, however, dip into the variations below. Serve with a nice crusty loaf of bread and a salad. Perfect for brunch or dinner.

SERVES 4

olive oil

80g morel or chestnut mushrooms, torn or sliced into bite-sized pieces

1 leek, white and pale green parts finely chopped

200g fresh asparagus spears; snap off woody ends (save them for stock) and cut on the diagonal into 3cm pieces

sea salt and black pepper

3 large eggs

50g fontina, Taleggio or mozzarella cheese, torn into bite-sized pieces

2 OF YOUR 5 A DAY WHEN SERVED WITH A SALAD OR A 150ML GLASS OF JUICE

Preheat the oven grill to high. Splash a glug of olive oil in an ovenproof 20cm frying pan over medium heat. Add the mushrooms and cook until they start to pick up a bit of colour. Add the leeks and asparagus and cook until they've softened up. Season. Take off the heat.

Whisk the eggs, just until incorporated. Season. Gently tip the eggs into the frying pan. Tilt, if needed, to disperse the egg over the veg. Dot the cheese over the top. Pop the frittata under the grill and cook for 10–12 minutes until it is puffed and the cheese is golden. Let it cool for 5 minutes.

Cut into wedges and serve with a salad, bread and a jug of juice.

SEASONAL VARIATIONS

SUMMER: caramelise 2 finely chopped onions. Fold 1 coarsely grated courgette through the onion before adding the egg. Sprinkle grated cheddar over the top.

AUTUMN: sauté a 250g mix of wild mushrooms with garlic and thyme. Add the egg and dot with hunks of a soft, goat's cheese.

WINTER: gently sauté a large handful of finely chopped kale with a clove of garlic and a pinch of dried chilli. Add the egg. Dot with 50g crumbled feta cheese and cook as above.

Egg-fried rice

Fried rice is one of those dishes you can chuck loads of veg into. I normally use it as a fridge-clearing dish, and I always try to get a variety of five different vegetables in there.

This is a spring version, making the most of fresh asparagus and broad beans. You can swap these with any seasonal veg you have to hand.

SERVES 4

a splash of olive oil

8 spring onions, 1 small onion or 1 leek, chopped

2 garlic cloves, finely chopped

2cm piece of fresh ginger, peeled and grated

1 chilli, deseeded and chopped

2 carrots, finely diced

160g asparagus, cut into 2cm pieces

160g broad beans, podded and slipped out of their outer skins

160g fresh or frozen peas

3 eggs, whisked

800g cooked long-grain rice (ideally cold leftovers but fresh is fine)

OPTIONAL FINISHING TOUCHES

a splash of soy sauce

a drizzle of sesame oil

a handful of basil, coriander, mint and/or beansprouts

a handful of toasted sesame seeds or cashew nuts

2.5 OF YOUR 5 A DAY

Put the wok on a high heat; leave until it's smoking. Add a splash of oil, sizzle for a few seconds, then add the onion or leek, garlic, ginger and chilli. Stir-fry for a moment, then add the carrots (and any other firm seasonal veg).

Stir-fry for 2 minutes, then add the asparagus, broad beans and peas (or any other soft seasonal veg). Cook for another 1–2 minutes. Scrape the contents of the wok into a bowl, then return the wok to the heat.

Add another splash of oil, swirl it around, then scramble the eggs. Use a wooden spoon or chopstick to stir until just set. Quickly add the rice and stir-fry, scraping in any egg that sticks to the sides, for a further 2–3 minutes to mix and heat through thoroughly.

Return the vegetables to the pan. Stir-fry for 1–2 minutes, to fold and warm through. Add any finishing touches and serve. Great with a pot of green tea (an energising hangover cure!).

Egyptian carrot and watercress salad
with poached egg and crispy leeks

There's no dish that celebrates eggs more than one crowned with a poached egg just awaiting the pierce of a fork to release its warm golden yolk. When perched upon a salad, the dribbling yolk creates the most regal dressing.

SERVES 4

4 tablespoons pine nuts

4 tablespoons sesame seeds

1½ teaspoons cumin seed

a few glugs of olive oil

4 slices of sourdough or rye, torn into 2cm hunks

500g slender carrots, larger ones halved lengthwise

3 garlic cloves, peeled and chopped

1 red chilli, finely chopped (use less for a milder dish)

sea salt and freshly ground pepper

a handful of fresh mint leaves, chopped

1 leek, cut into wispy 4cm-long slivers

4 large handfuls watercress

1 lemon

1 tablespoon white wine vinegar

4 eggs

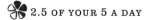 2.5 OF YOUR 5 A DAY

Place a large lidded frying pan over medium-high heat. Add the pine nuts, sesame seeds and cumin seeds. Toast until golden and fragrant. Spoon into a dish and set aside.

Place the pan back on the heat and splash in some olive oil. Add the torn bread hunks. Season with salt and cook until golden. Spoon the croûtons into a dish with the spicy seed mix.

Brush the pan clean and add more oil. Toss the carrots in, pop a lid on and fry over medium heat, shaking from time to time, until the carrots are softened and start to get crisp and golden around the edges.

Remove the lid and add the garlic and chilli. Fry until softened. Season. Take off the heat, dust the seed mix over and toss to coat. Divide between plates and sprinkle the fried bread over.

Rinse the pan and wipe it clean. Set over high heat. Add another good splash of oil. Once hot, add the leek strands to the pan. Lower the heat a bit and fry until just golden and starting to crisp. Season with salt then spoon onto a clean cloth to blot dry.

Fill a pot with water deep enough to cover the eggs. Add the vinegar, which prevents the egg white from spreading. Bring to a gentle simmer. Gently slip the eggs into the water, one by one. Cook at a soft simmer for 3–4 minutes, depending on how soft you want the yolk. Remove the eggs with a slotted spoon and set on a clean cloth to catch excess water.

Top each mound of carrots with the mint leaves and a handful of watercress. Squeeze the lemon juice over. Perch an egg on each salad and season. Finish with a nest of crispy leeks and serve.

Mushrooms on toast with a spiced fried egg

A fried egg is big, bold and generous, especially when it's perched on a heap of meaty mushrooms, drizzled with a chilli-spiked oil. It's a fabulous way to enjoy a well-sourced egg any time of the day.

SERVES 2

olive oil

250g mushrooms of your choice, sliced or torn

sea salt and black pepper

2 garlic cloves, finely chopped

3 tablespoons balsamic vinegar

a handful of parsley and/or basil, leaves finely chopped

¼ teaspoon chilli flakes, or finely chopped fresh chilli

4 slices of toast from a good loaf

2 large eggs

½ lemon

2.5 OF YOUR 5 A DAY WHEN SERVED WITH A 150ML GLASS OF JUICE

Place a large frying pan over medium-high heat. Add a splash of olive oil an add the mushrooms when it's hot. Season and sizzle until golden, adding more oil if needed.

Stir in the garlic, bar a pinch. Let it soften for a few minutes. Splash in the balsamic vinegar. Season.

Mix the reserved garlic and the chilli, then set aside. Fold the herbs through the warm mushrooms. Pile onto the toasts and keep warm.

Rinse and wipe the frying pan and place it over a medium-high heat. Add a splash of oil and carefully crack your eggs into the pan. Cook the eggs over a low heat for 2–3 minutes. Pop a lid on to help set the yolks a bit, if needed. Carefully spoon onto the mushroom-laden toasts.

Place the pan back on the heat and tip in the chilli and garlic mixture. Add a pinch of salt. Sizzle the oil for a moment. Spoon over the eggs. Serve.

VARIATIONS

SPANISH TOMATO BREAD WITH A SPICED FRIED EGG

Follow the instructions above but instead of mushrooms, use 250g halved cherry tomatoes. Sautée until softened, rather than golden, and add the garlic and balsamic vinegar (or use sherry vinegar) as above.

ASPARAGUS ON TOAST WITH SAFFRON-CHILLI OIL

Swap the mushrooms for 250g asparagus. Stir-fry until softened, again adding garlic but instead of the balsamic add lemon juice and a bit of zest. Add a pinch of saffron to the chilli and herbs used to top the eggs.

Gypsy toast

AKA 'eggy bread' or 'French toast'. I haven't skimped on the eggs here and they really shine through, especially when married with a bit of vanilla. I have, however, swapped the milk that's typically used. In its place, I've offered a quick nut milk, which takes a minute to make and gives you a delicious handful of chopped nuts to sprinkle over the top of your toast.

SERVES 4

100g almonds or hazelnuts

250ml water

4 eggs

½ vanilla pod, beans scraped, or a drop of vanilla extract (optional)

a dash of ground cinnamon

4–8 thick slices of bread from a good loaf

75ml honey, maple syrup or agave nectar

olive or nut oil

seasonal fruit, see below

2.5 OF YOUR 5 A DAY WHEN SERVED WITH A 150ML GLASS OF JUICE

Put the nuts in a blender with the water and blitz until they are finely chopped and you have a pale latte-coloured liquid. Strain, pressing the nut milk out and pour into a shallow bowl. Keep the nuts — you'll need to fry them with honey to top the toast.

Whisk the eggs with the nutty milk, vanilla (if using) and cinnamon. Press the bread into the mixture; you'll probably need to do this in batches. Let the bread soak for 3–5 minutes on each side, or until nicely softened. Pierce with a fork to help the bread soak up more of the mix.

Start cooking the toast while the other batches soak. Simply fry the slices in a splash of oil until golden on each side.

When cooked, tip the chopped nuts into the pan and lightly toast. Add the fruit and honey and cook until the fruit is just softened. Ladle this over the toasts and eat.

SEASONAL FRUIT

Select one of the following:

4 apples or pears, cored and sliced

6 plums, stoned and sliced

350g fresh berries

4 segmented oranges

4 bananas

8 dried apricots, thinly sliced

Apple and blueberry pancakes

The milk typically called for in pancake recipes can easily be swapped.
I discovered this when my son had a bad reaction to cow's milk as a baby.
I used apple juice instead and now I actually prefer it to milk. It lends a subtle
sweetness, which means you don't need to add sugar to the batter. It also
packs in a portion of fruit.

SERVES 4; MAKES 8–12
PANCAKES

2 eggs

225g wholegrain flour

3 teaspoons baking
powder

300ml apple juice

½ vanilla pod, seeds
scraped or 1 teaspoon
vanilla extract (optional)

1 tablespoon olive oil, plus
extra for cooking

TO SERVE

400g fresh blueberries

maple syrup or honey

❀ 2 OF YOUR 5 A DAY,
ADD A GLASS OF JUICE TO
DRINK TO INCREASE THIS
TO 3

Whisk the eggs until frothy. Add the remaining ingredients. Stir until you have a smooth batter.

Place a large frying pan, or two smaller ones, over medium-high heat. When the pan is hot, drizzle a little oil in the pan. Rotate or use a pastry brush to spread the oil evenly in the pan.

Dollop 2 dessertspoons of batter for each pancake (make them smaller or larger, if you like). Reduce the heat a bit and cook pancakes until you can see little bubbles working their way from the outside to the centre. Once they reach the centre, the pancake is set and ready to flip. Cook for a minute or two on the other side. Don't be tempted to press the pancake into the pan – it will squash out the air bubbles that make it light and fluffy.

Pile the warm pancakes on to the plates. Add a touch of butter, if you like, although I find cooking them in olive oil sort of gives them the flavour and moisture you'd get from a dab of butter.

Tumble the blueberries on top and drizzle with syrup.

Easy breakfasts without eggs or dairy

Breakfast is probably the easiest meal of the day to trim back on meat, eggs and dairy. While I love bacon, boiled eggs and yogurts for breakfast, I try to start a few days of the week on a lighter note.

The following recipes are completely plant-based. So, if you want to stick with nutritional and environmental recommendations to trim back on the amount of food from animals you eat, these recipes offer a great start.

Soaked oats with coconut milk

This is a twist on the classic Bircher Muesli. Piling the ingredients in an old jam jar makes it instantly portable, meaning that you can throw it in your bag before you dash off to work – just make sure the lid's on tight!

SERVES 1

rolled oats

1 tablespoon dried fruit, snipped into 1cm pieces

1 tablespoon seeds or chopped nuts

a pinch of ground cinnamon, cardamom and/or vanilla seeds

apple or orange juice

a handful of fresh fruit

coconut milk

 2 OF YOUR 5 A DAY

Fill a jam jar half full with oats. Add dried fruit (raisins, chopped apricots, dates...) and seeds or nuts. Add the spice. Stir through.

Top the oats with juice. Stir. Add a little more juice if the oats look dry.

Put the lid on. Store in the fridge overnight or make in the morning before you go to work – the oats should be soft enough by the time you get to your desk.

Dollop coconut milk over the top and eat a handful of fresh fruit.

Coconut pancakes

Coconut milk has the right amount of fat and protein to do the binding that eggs do in most baking. These pancakes sre slightly denser but the difference is not dramatic, and they're really delicious – especially with a hint of cardamom.

SERVES 4

225g kamut or wholewheat flour

3 teaspoons baking powder

3 cardamom pods, crushed and seeds ground

250ml coconut milk

1 tablespoon honey or maple syrup, plus extra to serve

2 tablespoons olive oil, plus extra for cooking

150ml water

8 plums or 4 bananas

 1 OF YOUR 5 A DAY

Mix all the ingredients (except the fruit) together. Whisk until you have a smooth batter. If it's too thick, add a drizzle of water. If it's too thin, add more flour. You want the batter to be the consistency of double cream – it should dollop, not pour.

Warm a pan over medium-high heat. Brush with oil. Add two dessertspoons of batter at a time. When it has little air bubbles coming through in the centre, it's ready to flip.

Cook on the other side for a minute or two. Keep in a warm place until you've cooked the remaining pancakes. Serve with sliced plums or bananas and honey or maple syrup.

You can freeze any leftover pancakes. Wrap individually and just pop them into a toaster from frozen until warmed through.

Dairy alternatives

One tricky thing to avoid at breakfast time is milk. It's poured over cereal, splashed into tea and soaked into porridge oats. Here are a few tasty alternatives. They also work well in baking.

Nut milks

You can make nut milk from just about any nut: almonds, hazelnuts, brazil nuts, cashew and macadamia nuts are my favourites.

Taste: slightly sweet and nutty, obviously.

Consistency: quite thin like skim milk.

Use: best for baking, pouring over cereal or in smoothies and milkshakes. Lovely whipped up with frozen banana.

Bonus: you have leftover nuts, which you can use in a number of recipes:

Chocolate Banana Bread, PAGE 215

Soaked Oats, PAGE 179

Rice Pudding with Seasonal Fruit, PAGES 212-213

To make: measure 1 part nuts to 2 parts water. So, for 500ml of milk, you'll need 250g nuts and 500ml water.

Put the nuts and water into a blender or a food-processor and blitz until the nuts are finely chopped.

Place a sieve over a jug and strain the nuts from the milk, pressing as much milk out of them as possible.

For a creamier milk, soak the nuts in the water overnight.

You can freeze both the milk and the chopped nuts, or store in the fridge for 2–3 days.

Oat milk

Taste: toasty and comforting.

Consistency: thicker than nut milk but a bit floury.

Use: lovely to drink or for use in smoothies or milkshakes.

Bonus: you're left with soaked oats, which you can mix with fruit and yogurt, coconut milk or cashew cream (below) to make a delicious breakfast.

To make: Just blend 1 part oats to 2 parts water. Strain the oats from the liquid, pressing them to extract as much oat milk as possible.

Try adding a bit of vanilla or cinnamon to the oats and water before blending. It's also delicious when mixed with a nut milk. It makes for a nice balance of flavours and textures.

Cashew cream

Cashew nuts are wonderfully smooth and creamy. Ground and whipped with water, they make a great alternative to cream.

There's a brand called Booja-Booja which makes ice cream out of cashew nuts and it's absolutely delicious. They simply use cashews, water, agave syrup and vanilla beans. However, it takes quite a bit of work to whip up enough cashew cream to make a tub of ice cream. So make small batches

as an alternative to yogurt for topping the Soaked Oats on page 179, or to stir into curries, such as the Chicken, Coconut and Butternut Squash Curry on page 61.

To make: just blend 1 part cashews to 1½ parts water. Blitz until the nuts are finely ground. Scrape everything through a sieve until you have a fairly thick cream. For a smoother cream, soak the cashews overnight.

Apple-sweetened granola with almond milk

The sweetness in this granola comes mostly from fruit. There's only a modest amount of honey and absolutely no sugar. It has loads of toasty almonds running through it, as well – they're added to the granola after you've used them to make vanilla almond milk, which complements the granola.

ENOUGH GRANOLA AND MILK FOR 4

200g almonds

500ml water

seeds from ½ vanilla pod

250g rolled oats

1 teaspoon ground cinnamon

100g seeds (sunflower, pumpkin and/or sesame)

75ml apple juice

4 tablespoons honey

3 tablespoons olive oil

6 tablespoons dried fruit

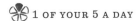 1 OF YOUR 5 A DAY

First make the milk. Put the almonds, vanilla seeds and water in a blender or a food-processor. Blend until the nuts are fully ground and you have a latte-coloured liquid. Strain through a fine sieve. Pour the milk into a bottle and refrigerate until ready to serve (up to 3 days). Reserve the ground almonds.

Preheat the oven to 160°C/gas mark 3.

Mix the ground almonds with the oats, cinnamon and seeds. Drizzle the apple juice, honey and olive oil over. Fold to mix.

Scatter in a thin layer over a baking sheet. Cook for 45–60 minutes, turning the mix often, until golden.

Once it's cooked, fold the dried fruit through. Let it cool before serving. Serve with the cold almond milk.

Apples and pears with tahini dip

This easy-to-make dip is perfect for autumn apples and pears. It also works well on toast with slices of banana on top.

SERVES 4

6 tablespoons tahini

4–6 tablespoons water

2 tablespoons honey

1 teaspoon ground cinnamon (optional)

4 apples and 4 pears

 2 OF YOUR 5 A DAY

Place the tahini in a bowl. Whisk in the water little by little. Fold in the honey and cinnamon.

Slice the apples and pears just before serving. Dip in.

Raspberry chocolate spread

If you love pain au chocolat, or chocolate spread on toast, here's a delightful alternative. The raspberries whipped into the mix add a wonderful freshness, as well as a portion of fruit. It's perfect on warm bread.

ENOUGH CHOCOLATE SPREAD FOR 4

100g fresh raspberries

200g dark chocolate, roughly chopped or broken

125ml coconut milk

❀ 2 OF YOUR 5 A DAY IF SERVED WITH A BOWL OF FRUIT

Crush the raspberries until they're a puréed mush. Do this with a fork or a wooden spoon.

Place a frying pan over medium heat. Place a metal or glass bowl on top of the pan (this will gently warm the bowl and the chocolate inside – it's a simpler take on the bain marie). Add the chocolate and coconut milk to the bowl.

Gently stir the contents as it warms, until all the chocolate has just melted. Remove from the heat. Fold the raspberries through. Cool and serve with hunks or slices of sourdough or any other good bread.

The spread can be made up to one day in advance.

Honey berry jam

I'm hopeless at making jam, probably because my jaw always drops when I see how much sugar you're supposed to add and I start trying to scale it down. It never works.

But this works – and it doesn't contain a speckle of sugar. It also only takes 5–10 minutes to make, and it offers a portion of fruit.

ENOUGH FOR 4 SLABS OF TOAST

400g strawberries, raspberries and/or blackberries

2 tablespoons honey

❀ 1 OF YOUR 5 A DAY

Squish the berries in a bowl using the bottom of a glass, a wooden spoon or a fork. Stir the honey in. Place in a frying pan over medium-high heat and cook for 5–10 minutes, until all the water has cooked out and you have a fairly thick jam. It will still be a bit runny but it will thicken up as it cools.

Delicious served warm or cold on toast drizzled with olive or a nutty almond or hazelnut oil.

Will keep in the fridge, in a jar, for 3 days.

Buttery avocado toast

Avocados are such an amazing, versatile fruit, and they're delicious for breakfast. They're also so creamy and buttery in their own right that you don't need a slick of butter on your toast. Just a drizzle of olive oil over the top.

FOR EACH PERSON, YOU NEED

a thick slice of bread from a good loaf (a seeded wholegrain bread works nicely here)

olive oil

½ ripe avocado

sea salt and black pepper

a wedge of lemon

2 teaspoons sunflower seeds, toasted

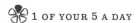 1 OF YOUR 5 A DAY

Lightly toast your bread. Drizzle with olive oil.

Scoop the avocado out and spread over the toast. Season. Squeeze lemon juice over the top and add a splash a bit of olive oil and finish with a dusting of toasted seeds. Delicious.

Spanish tomato bread

In Spain and other Mediterranean countries such as Malta, they love starting the day with thick slabs of bread weighed down with olive oil and tomatoes. It's quick, healthy and absolutely delicious.

FOR EACH SERVING, YOU NEED

2 regular tomatoes or 10 cherry tomatoes

½ garlic clove, finely minced (optional)

sea salt

olive oil

1 thick slice sourdough, or any other good bread

 2 OF YOUR 5 A DAY

Preheat the oven to 200°C/gas mark 6.

Dice the tomato. Mix with the garlic, if using, and a pinch of salt.

Drizzle olive oil over the bread. Place on a baking tray and pile the tomato on top. Pop in the oven for 8–10 minutes, just until the bread and tomatoes are warm. Delicious.

DAIRY

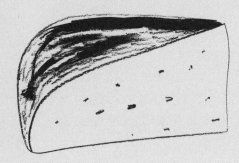

The vitamin content of milk gets stretched when cows are bred to produce more milk. So, large dairies may be giving us more milk but its nutritional value is diluted.

The salty morishness offered by a hunk of cheddar, the comfort of warm frothy milk in coffee, the seductive charm of creamy vanilla ice cream: dairy is so wonderfully consoling. Milk, after all, is the first food we consume. I adore it but there's an enormous pressure on dairy farmers to produce more and more of it for us at lower and lower prices. As a result, both cows and dairy farmers are suffering.

In the 1960s, your average dairy cow produced a little more than 3,500 litres of milk a year. Now, cows are delivering up to 10,000 litres or more per year – that's about 200 litres each week from just one cow. If she were just feeding her calf, she'd only need to produce 28 litres of milk each week. This sort of milk is not good for us. One American dairy farmer admitted: 'We're mining the cow'.

Each week, nine dairy farmers go out of business in Britain. In the 1920s there were 150,000 farmers producing milk in the British Isles. Now, there are only 15,000. Those who are producing milk are getting less money for it. In Britain, the price farmers got for milk fell by a quarter over the decade leading up to 2004. As a result, we're losing family dairy farms. In their place, enormous so-called 'mega dairies' are emerging. This story is not unique to Britain. In America, large-scale dairies are now the norm.

While I was writing this book, an industrialised dairy operation was being mapped out for the English countryside. Set to be the largest dairy unit in western Europe, the plan was to establish a 22-acre farm, housing 8,100 cows in eight sheds. The sheds did have open access at the sides but for the most part, these cows would spend their days indoors. Their feed would primarily consist of locally-grown maize, not grass.

To put this in context, the farmer who I buy my milk from has a 110-strong herd of rare-breed Guernsey cows with 220 acres of land to graze. Nick Gosling's cows eat mostly grass, and he and his wife Christine know their individual names. His milk is just a few pennies more expensive than what I would pay in the supermarket. But a pint of his milk is still cheaper than a pack of chewing gum.

Milk and other dairy products have been relegated to mere commodities, consumed without much thought. When we treat food like this, it becomes financially more difficult for farmers and producers to continue with love and care for their craft.

Patrick Holden, the former director of the Soil Association, and dairy farmer himself, said 'You can't just blame the supermarkets, that is pointless. The choice is with us, the customers: it's we who have to change the way we buy. So we farmers must help the public to relearn where milk comes from, to value it and the animals, the land and the people that produced it.'

If you eat and drink dairy, a wonderful move you could make is to try to source it from a farmer you know by name. Learn his or her story. Go to their farm. A farm with an open-door policy is always a good sign.

And don't skimp on the fat. If you're buying dairy from grass-fed cows, the fat in their products is where the concentration of heart-healthy omega 3 is found. So skip the skimmed and semi-skimmed. Full-fat is where it's at.

Every day 260,000 packs of cheese and 1.3 million yogurts are thrown away in Britain.

A cheesemonger's lunch

This is not a strict and structured recipe. The idea here is to wander into a cheese shop, talk to the owner, linger amongst the smells and stunning craftsmanship, and then pick up one really amazing cheese and a colourful bouquet of seasonal fruits, nuts, and vegetables. When you get home, lay it all out on a board, along with a good loaf or a quick homemade batch of Rustic Oatcakes (see below).

This book is all about savouring the foods with a story and truly appreciating them. There's no better way to do it than by enjoying their purest state. An artfully made cheese paired with well-sourced seasonal produce illustrates this notion beautifully.

CHEESEBOARD IDEAS

SOFT, WASHED-RIND CHEESES
Famous varieties include brie and camembert, but seek out unusual and local versions.
Lovely in the spring with... asparagus, sprouting broccoli, strawberries, spring lettuce, new potatoes

FRESH CHEESES
Famous varieties: chèvre blanc, ricotta, feta
Perfect in the summer with... ripe tomatoes, olives, breadsticks, melon, peaches, cucumber, radishes

SEMI-HARD, AGED CHEESES
Famous varieties include Cheddar, Manchego, Comté
Cherish in the autumn with... apples, pears, figs, grapes, fresh walnuts, quince, rustic oatcakes

BLUE CHEESE
Famous varieties include Stilton, Gorgonzola, Roquefort...
Wonderful in the winter with... celery, chestnuts, dates, clementines, pomegranate, a nice crusty loaf

RUSTIC OATCAKES

Preheat the oven to 180°C/gas mark 4. Mix together 75g stoneground oats, 75g rolled oats, 2 tablespoons sunflower or sesame seeds (optional), a pinch of salt, 2 tablespoons olive oil and 2 teaspoons runny honey. Rub in until the oats feel a bit like wet sand. Add 50ml hot water, mixing through until the oats start to come together. Add more oats (either variety) if it's too wet, more water if it's too dry.

Squeeze and press the oat mixture until it starts to come together. Tip on to a cutting board and shape into a stumpy log-shape, about 3–4cm in diameter and about 8cm long. Slice into 10–12 thin rounds. Place on an oiled baking sheet. Press each slice a bit flatter and tidy up the sides.

Carefully transfer the oatcakes to an oiled baking tray. Bake for 12–15 minutes, or until golden.

The same creamy sauce but less work, and better for you. Here are three fresh, veg-loaded takes on a classic.

Roasted butternut, leek and mascarpone

The beauty of this dish is that you get a voluptuous sauce by simply stirring dollops of creamy mascarpone through the warmed pasta. It's much easier than making a classic cheese sauce, and it's a much lighter option.

SERVES 4

1 large butternut squash, peeled and cut into chunky dice

olive oil

sea salt and freshly ground pepper

3 leeks, whites and light greens sliced about 1cm thick

3 garlic cloves, crushed and peeled

a few sprigs of thyme

300g pasta (large shells or tubes work best)

200g mascarpone

a large handful of wild rocket leaves

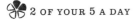 2 OF YOUR 5 A DAY

Preheat the oven to 200°C/gas mark 6. Tumble the butternut squash into a roasting dish. Drizzle a bit of olive oil over the top, season and shake to mix. Pop it into the oven for 20 minutes. Add the leeks, garlic and thyme and continue roasting for 15–20 minutes, until the squash is soft and starting to pick up colour.

Cook your pasta, then drain and drizzle some olive oil over. Return to the pot and stir in the mascarpone until well mixed. Add the squash, leeks and rocket. Fold through and serve.

Broccoli, blue cheese and walnut breadcrumbs

This buttery blue cheese sauce is heavenly and it works so well with broccoli.
The toasty walnut breadcrumbs dusted over the top are a style of Italian pan
grattato. They offer an earthy contrast to the richness of the cheese.

olive oil

2 garlic cloves, finely chopped

75g breadcrumbs

75g walnuts, finely chopped

300g pasta (rigatoni or spaghetti works well here)

1 head broccoli, cut into small florets

50g unsalted butter

150g Dolcelatte or Gorgonzola

sea salt and black pepper

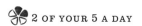 2 OF YOUR 5 A DAY

Place the empty frying pan over a medium heat. Add a splash of olive oil. Sauté the garlic until tender. Add the breadcrumbs and walnuts and cook until nicely golden. Set aside.

Cook your pasta. Add the broccoli halfway through the cooking, so that it cooks for 3–5 minutes. Drain. Add a splash of olive oil.

Rinse the pan, wipe clean and place back on the heat. Add the butter and cheese. Stir until the cheese has just melted.

Add the pasta and broccoli and gently fold through, then pile onto plates. Sprinkle the garlic walnut breadcrumbs over the top and serve.

Courgette, Parmesan cream and pine nuts

This is so rich and creamy that you'll find it hard to believe it's better for you
than your average plate of macaroni cheese. It's also subtly loaded with
two portions of vegetables per serving. And it only takes 15 minutes to make.

SERVES 4

300g pasta (penne works well)

olive oil

50g pine nuts

4 courgettes, cut into 1cm thick pieces

2 garlic cloves, finely chopped

175ml double cream

25g Parmesan, finely grated

sea salt and black pepper

a handful of fresh basil, chopped

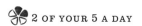 2 OF YOUR 5 A DAY

Cook the pasta, then drain. Drizzle the pasta with olive oil while still in the colander.

Place the pasta pan back on the heat. When it's warm, add the pine nuts and toast them. Tip them in with the pasta. Return the pan to the hob and add a glug of olive oil. When it's hot, add the courgettes. Season and cook until they start to pick up colour. Stir the garlic through and sauté until it softens.

Add the pasta to the pan, along with the cream and Parmesan, and fold them through. Remove from the heat. Season. Serve with a sprinkling of fresh basil on top.

If you're new to risotto, don't go turning the page thinking that they're too complicated or take hours to make. Thirty minutes and a handful of ingredients is all it takes. It's so simple.

Risotto – the canvas

Here is the basic formula for making a good risotto. It's so easy that my three-year-old son can almost master this.

On the following page are various vegetable and cheese pairings. A lot of risotto recipes will just call for the addition of Parmesan, but all sorts of different cheeses can be used to make the dish more interesting.

SERVES 4

olive oil

1 onion, finely chopped

200g risotto rice

175ml wine or sherry (optional — it adds heaps of flavour but you can make a decent risotto without it)

200g of a seasonal vegetable, finely diced

sea salt and black pepper

1 litre chicken or veg stock, simmering

150g cheese

1 OF YOUR 5 A DAY,
2.5 WHEN PAIRED WITH
A VEGETABLE SIDE

Place a large pot over medium heat. Add a splash of olive oil. Once hot, add the onion and gently sauté for 10–15 minutes.

Add the risotto rice and let it crackle and pop in the pan for a few minutes. Splash in the wine and let it bubble up until the rice has guzzled it up.

Stir in the veg of your choice, add a good grinding of pepper and cook for a minute or two before adding your first ladle of stock.

Set a timer for 20 minutes and continue to feed the stock to the rice little by little until the timer goes off.

Fold in the cheese and a good pinch of salt. Add a tiny bit more stock, if needed. You want your risotto to have a nice creamy texture and not be too thick.

Pile on to plates and finish with a glug of oil and Parmesan, toasted nuts or breadcrumbs, if you like.

Risotto – vegetable palette

BEETROOT

Children love this one as it turns the rice pink. Peel and finely dice 1 large beetroot or 2 smaller ones. Add it after the rice and wine, as instructed on page 193, and follow the recipe from there. Cheese-wise, fold in 125g of mascarpone and top with a 25g nugget of Parmesan cheese. Serve with roasted or steamed broccoli.

CAULIFLOWER

Cut the cauliflower florets and the stalk into 1–2cm hunks. Add after the rice and wine. Stir in 150g of a creamy blue cheese such as Dolcelatte or a salty blue such as Stilton.

Finish with fried breadcrumbs dusted over the top. Serve with a side of spinach or a salad of shaved beetroot, fennel and avocado.

BROAD BEANS

Fresh summer broad beans make a deliciously nutty addition to risotto. Take them out of their pods and slip each bean out of its white coating. Add after the rice and wine. Fold in 150g of mild goat or sheep's milk cheese at the end.

Sprinkle finely chopped fresh rosemary over the top. Serve with pan-fried carrots tossed in balsamic vinegar.

CELERY

Finely diced celery is delicious in risotto. Add after the rice and wine step.

Fold 125g mascarpone and 25g Parmesan through at the end. Finish with basil and mint leaves. Serve with a salad of crunchy raw peas, radishes and colourful leaves.

PARSNIP

Peel and dice the parsnip. Add after the rice and wine. Try lamb or rabbit stock in the risotto. Fold 50g grated Parmesan through.

Finish with 100g (3–4 rashers) grilled and crumbled, or sliced, bacon over the top. Pair with a salad of leaves and orange segments.

PUMPKIN

Use a sweet sherry instead of wine and finish with a nutty butter, made by gently frying 100g butter until it turns a frothy, golden brown. Fold a few handfuls of rocket or cavolo nero through the risotto. Dust 50g finely grated Parmesan and a handful of toasted hazelnuts over the top.

Arancini

Arancini are little balls of breadcrumb-coated and cheese-filled risotto. It's essential that you use cold, leftover risotto to make them. Otherwise, they just fall apart. So when I make a risotto, I always allow for extras.

Don't worry about weights and measurements in this recipe. Just bish, bash, bosh it together. It'll be delicious.

I'm usually satisfied with one arancini, served with a big salad, but one could easily snaffle two of them.

SERVES 1–4, DEPENDING ON HOW MUCH LEFTOVER RISOTTO YOU HAVE

FOR EACH ARANCINI, YOU NEED:

two handfuls of breadcrumbs

a handful of cold, leftover risotto

a little marble-sized nugget of cheese

olive or sunflower oil

2 OF YOUR 5 A DAY WHEN SERVED WITH A SALAD

Place the breadcrumbs on a plate. Roughly shape and squeeze the risotto into spheres the size of golf balls. Place in the centre of the breadcrumbs, then flatten and press into 1cm-thick patties. Sit a nugget of cheese in the centre of each, then fold the risotto up, over and around it. Roll the risotto in the breadcrumbs to coat, and form it into a ball.

Pour a good few glugs of oil into a frying pan — you want a 1–2cm layer of oil. Place over medium heat. Once hot, shallow fry the arancini until golden all over. Drain in a colander or on a stale piece of bread to soak up some of the oil.

SERVING SUGGESTIONS

A big salad with dressed with a Chilli Balsamic Vinaigrette, PAGE 127

Broccoli with Toasted Almonds, PAGE 116

Rolling-pin ravioli with pumpkin and sage butter

*I always find that cheese gets lost when it's tucked inside a ravioli parcel. So,
these ones are packed with the pure taste of pumpkin and garlic. That means
you can drizzle a generous gloss of sage butter over the top and finish with a
dusting of Parmesan. The flavours are much more prominent.*

**SERVES 4, MAKING 8–10 RAVIOLI
FOR EACH PERSON**

FOR THE FILLING

1 small to medium-sized
pumpkin or butternut squash

2 garlic cloves, roughly
chopped

sea salt and black pepper

FOR THE PASTA DOUGH

230g plain flour

½ teaspoon salt

2 eggs

1 tablespoon olive oil

4 tablespoons water

FOR THE SAGE BUTTER

75g butter

a small handful of sage leaves,
finely chopped (about 1 heaped
tablespoon)

sea salt

3 tablespoons pine nuts,
toasted

TO SERVE

400g baby leaf spinach

2 garlic cloves, roughly
chopped

sea salt and black pepper

25g Parmesan cheese, finely
grated

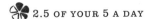 2.5 OF YOUR 5 A DAY

First make the filling. Roast, steam or sauté the squash with garlic until
tender. Mash or whizz in a blender to a smooth purée. If it looks a bit
wet, put it in a saucepan and simmer until the water evaporates out and
the squash looks thick and rich. Season well and set aside.

For the pasta, tip the flour and salt into a large bowl. Make a well and
break the eggs into the centre. Add the oil and water, and fold together,
mixing to form a soft dough. Add drops of water if it's too dry or more
flour if it's too sticky. Knead on a floured surface until smooth and
elastic. Quarter the dough. Roll on a floured surface until ¼–½cm thick.
Cut into 2–3cm diameter rounds using a shotglass, small jar or a
cutter. Press each round a bit thinner using the heel of your hand.
Pair the circles.

Now fill the ravioli: brush one of the circles in each pair with water. Add
1 teaspoon of filling. Top with the other circle and seal, pressing the
sides together and drawing out any air pockets. Continue with
remaining dough. Dust the ravioli with plenty of flour to keep them dry
and prevent them from sticking. Place on a baking sheet and cover with
a dry cloth.

Let the ravioli sit while you wilt the spinach. Place the spinach, garlic
and a pinch of salt in a large lidded pot over medium-low heat and let it
wilt down – no water or oil needed at this stage. Once the spinach has
cooked down, tip it into a colander and gently press out the bitter juices.
Add a splash of oil and fluff through. Season and set aside.

Place the butter in a small pan and let it cook slowly until frothy and
lightly browned. Add the sage and a good pinch of salt. Set aside.

Cook the ravioli: bring a very large pot of salted water to the boil. Cook
in batches for 3–5 minutes, until glossy and cooked through. Use a
slotted spoon to remove each batch to a warm tray and drizzle with oil.

Arrange the ravioli on the plates. Dot the spinach around them. Gently
reheat the butter, spoon over the ravioli and scatter Parmesan over top.

Pizza party

Pizza has a lot going for it. It's convivial. Everyone loves it. You can pile a good bit of veg on top, and you don't need mountains of cheese or meat to make a fine pizza, especially when you're using a top-notch cheese or sausage.

SERVES 4–6

THE DOUGH

1 x 7g packet dried yeast or 3 rounded teaspoons fresh yeast

4 tablespoons lukewarm water

500g strong white flour (if unavailable, use plain white flour)

225ml cool water

½ teaspoon salt, plus extra for topping

1 teaspoon sugar

4 tablespoons olive oil, plus extra for baking

TOMATO SAUCE FOR THE BASE

1 onion, finely chopped

olive oil

2 garlic cloves, roughly chopped

800g tinned chopped tomatoes

a splash of balsamic vinegar

a few roughly torn basil leaves

❀ 2 OF YOUR 5 A DAY

Preheat the oven to 200°C/gas mark 6 and place a large baking tray (or a pizza stone, if you have one) in the oven to warm through.

Place the yeast in a small bowl. Stir in the warm water until well mixed and let the yeast bubble up in a warm place for 10 minutes.

Tip the flour into a large mixing bowl. Add the cool water, salt, sugar and olive oil to the flour but don't mix just yet.

Add the watery yeast and give the dough a good mix, folding all the wet ingredients through. Knead the dough on a floured surface until smooth and elastic. Add a bit more flour if the dough is too wet. Let it rest in an oiled bowl for 30 minutes.

Meanwhile, make the tomato sauce. Sauté the onion in olive oil until soft. Add the garlic and cook for a few minutes longer. Add the tinned tomatoes and let the sauce bubble away on medium-high heat until it is really thick. Add the balsamic vinegar and basil leaves. Let it cool while you prepare the pizza bases.

Divide the dough into four or six balls. Roll on a floured surface into oblong or circular pizzas. Brush with oil on both sides, place on a preheated baking tray and cook in the oven for 10 minutes. Flip the dough, brush the top with more oil and slather with tomato sauce. Add toppings of your choice (see opposite) and bake.

NOTE the pizza dough freezes extremely well. Once you've divided the dough, wrap up each individual portion in clingfilm. Freeze for up to 6 months. It takes just 1 hour or so to defrost at room temperature, making it a great dinner option for last-minute guests.

Toppings

a little bit of cheese – or meat – and a lot of veg.

SAUSAGE WITH FENNEL, ONIONS, ROCKET, ARTICHOKES AND OLIVES

For each pizza, you'll want the meat from a small sausage. Remove it from the skin and pinch into little, rustic-looking meatballs. Fry in a touch of olive oil until just golden. Add some thinly sliced onions and cook in the fat and oil until soft. Pile them on top of your pizza. Finish with torn marinated artichoke hearts and a few shavings of fresh fennel (done by just shaving off thin slivers with a vegetable peeler). Dot with a few olives. Bake and finish with a handful of rocket, a drizzle of olive oil and a little grating of Parmesan.

COURGETTES, CAPERS, BASIL, CHERRY TOMATOES AND MOZZARELLA

Spread some tomato sauce over the base. Sprinkle over a little salt and some chopped garlic. Top with shavings of courgette, capers, torn hunks of mozzarella and cherry tomatoes. Bake until the tomatoes are nice and soft. Scatter a handful of fresh basil leaves over the pizza once it's cooked.

RED PEPPER RIBBONS, BROCCOLI, PINE NUTS AND GOAT'S CHEESE

Pop a whole red pepper in a hot oven for 30 minutes. Let it cool, remove the skin and tear into thin ribbons, discarding the seeds. Or you can cheat by using jars of roasted pepper. Quickly steam a few thinly sliced broccoli florets. Spread tomato sauce on the dough and scatter the broccoli and peppers over. Dot with a soft goat's cheese. Dust with pine nuts and bake until golden. A few raisins are also nice on this one.

PORCINI, PUMPKIN, CHESTNUT AND MASCARPONE

Stir a spoonful of mascarpone through your tomato sauce and spread on the dough. Top with shavings of raw porcini, pumpkin and peeled chestnuts – use a vegetable peeler or a fancy mandolin to create the shavings. Drizzle with olive oil, season and bake. Finish with a heap of rocket leaves and some Parmesan.

Greek feta wraps

Wrapping a traditional Greek salad up in flatbread or a tortilla wrap turns it into a deliciously filling meal. Seek out a top notch barrel-aged feta from Greece. Or, source a feta-style cheese made by a cheesemaker near you.

SERVES 4

500g ripe tomatoes – a mix of colours and styles is best

1 green pepper, halved and deseeded

1 small or ½ large cucumber, diced

1 red onion, sliced paper thin

a handful of Kalamata olives, roughly chopped

a sprinkle of capers (optional)

a few sprigs of fresh dill (optional)

1 tablespoon red wine vinegar

2 tablespoons olive oil

sea salt and black pepper

8 flat breads or homemade tortilla wraps (see below)

200g Greek feta

a handful of fresh mint leaves, roughly chopped

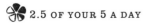 2.5 OF YOUR 5 A DAY

Slice the tomatoes and then roughly chop them so you have nice bite-sized pieces.

Thinly slice the green pepper into rings and then roughly chop them. Mix with the cucumber, onion, olives, capers (if using) and herbs.

Toss it all together with the vinegar, oil and seasoning. Divide between the open tortilla breads.

Crumble the feta on top, flip the bottom end up and roll up.

Lovely with fresh lemonade on ice with sprigs of mint.

HOMEMADE FLOUR TORTILLA WRAPS

Mix 175g plain white flour with 125g wholemeal flour. Add 1½ teaspoons baking powder, ½ teaspoon salt and 2 tablespoons olive oil. Slowly fold in 200ml warm (not boiling) water.

Stir until a loose, sticky ball is formed. Dust with flour and knead for a few minutes until the dough is soft yet firm. Pinch the dough into eight pieces. Roll each into a ball. Set a large frying pan over medium flame, allowing it to heat while you roll the tortillas.

On a floured surface, pat one of the dough balls into a 5cm circle. Roll out until it's about the size of a dinner plate. Cook the tortilla in the hot frying pan for about thirty seconds on each side. It should start to puff up a bit when it's done. Brush one side with olive oil to keep it moist. Wrap in a clean cloth as you cook the others.

Once you've cooked the full batch, eat straight away. Makes 8.

Beans on toast with melted cheddar

This is classic nursery fare. It's true, cure-the-blues comfort food, and the softly sweet, pillowy beans are a great foil for sharp farmhouse Cheddar. Find the best Cheddar you can and then whip up this quick recipe for homemade beans, supplied with thanks by Candy Delaney of Spoonfed Suppers.

SERVES 4–6

800g tinned cannellini beans

olive oil

2 small onions, finely chopped

2 sticks celery, finely diced

2 garlic cloves, crushed

2 tablespoons honey

800g tinned chopped tomatoes

2 tablespoons tomato purée

1 teaspoon fresh thyme leaves

8 slices wholegrain bread

200g good Cheddar cheese, grated

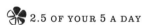 2.5 OF YOUR 5 A DAY

Empty the beans into a saucepan. Heat gently for 5 minutes, stirring frequently. Drain well.

Meanwhile, heat a splash of olive oil in a large saucepan and fry the onion, celery and garlic for 4 minutes, or until the onion starts to soften. Stir in the honey, tomatoes and tomato purée. Simmer for 2 minutes.

Fold the warmed beans and thyme through. Return to the heat and simmer for about 8 minutes, or until all the vegetables are soft and piping hot.

Brush the bread with olive oil, then toast under the grill. Pile on the beans and sprinkle with grated cheese. Pop the toast back in the grill until the cheese is bubbling and golden.

Ice cream parlour

A lot of the red-bordered features in this book address potential problem spots when it comes to eating less meat. This one highlights our weakness for ice cream, as its custard base is rich with both eggs and dairy – both of which fall into the 'eat less meat' equation.

Happily, I've created some truly scrumptious alternatives. They're rich with fruit – offering at least one portion – and they contain pretty much no sugar.

Chocolate monkey ice cream

When my bananas start to don black spots, I slip the skins off, break them into bite-sized hunks, freeze them in a plastic tub and use them to make this delicious, instant ice cream. Once your fridge is stocked with frozen banana hunks, you can whip this up during a commercial break if you're having a lazy evening on the sofa.

FOR A NICE BOWLFUL, YOU'LL NEED:

1 frozen banana, roughly chopped

10g dark chocolate, roughly chopped

1 heaped teaspoon peanut butter

a tiny pinch of sea salt

 1 OF YOUR 5 A DAY

Blitz all the ingredients in a food-processor until smooth and creamy.

Chocolate almond milkshake

This one's outrageously decadent. It's like a cold, creamy, melted chocolate almond bar.

FOR EACH MILKSHAKE, YOU'LL NEED:

2 tablespoons flaked almonds

20g dark chocolate, finely chopped

100ml cold water

1 frozen banana, roughly chopped

 1 OF YOUR 5 A DAY

Toast the almonds in a frying pan until golden. Place in a blender or food-processor while they're still warm. Add the chocolate and blend until the almonds are chopped and the chocolate is melted. Slowly drizzle the water in as you blend. Tip the frozen banana hunks into the mix. Blend well.

The milkshake will have little bits of toasted almond going through it. I like it this way but if you want a smoother texture, pass it through a sieve first to catch these out.

VARIATIONS

Mocha Milkshake Replace the almonds and water with 125ml warm (but not hot) coffee. Blend the coffee with the chocolate until the chocolate has melted. Add the bananas and whip until creamy.

Juicy ice lollies

I almost feel fraudulent for penning this as a recipe but if you've yet to think of this, it's great for children and adults to give it a go.

 1 LOLLY GIVES YOU 0.5 OF YOUR 5 A DAY

The instructions are in the title: juice + lolly mould + freezer = ice lolly.

That's it. Pour fresh juice into an ice lolly mould (or into a narrow, thin cup with a stick). Freeze. Voila. You have delicious ice lollies.

Making these is a great way to shift juice before it expires, or before you go on holiday.

All juices make delicious ice lollies. My favourites are: apple, apple with mango, orange, pineapple, and orange and raspberry juice. You can't go wrong with these.

Instant 100-per-cent fruit sorbets

Every time I whip up one of these I think they're too good to be true, as making sorbet in the traditional manner involves making a sugar syrup and lots of churning. But all you need to make a delicious sorbet is frozen fruit and a blender or food-processor.

To make a nice-sized scoop, you need 120g of fruit, which will give you 1.5 of your 5 A Day. Not bad!

RIPE MANGO

Peel and finely chop. Freeze. Whip until smooth. Delicious with chopped pistachio nuts and a drizzle of honey over the top.

RED GRAPES

This is really delicious. Just freeze whole grapes and whip them up once they're frozen. Add a drop of dessert wine, if you like.

PINEAPPLE

Cut into really small dice (1cm cubes). Freeze. Blend. For a twist, add vanilla seeds and a bit of finely chopped chilli before you blend.

STRAWBERRIES

Finely chop ripe berries. Freeze them, along with any accumulated juices. Whip in a blender or food-processor with a little drizzle of coconut milk or orange juice. Add vanilla seeds or rose water for added flavour. Fold a few spoonfuls of icing sugar through, if needed.

CHERRIES

Remove the stones and tear the cherries in half. Freeze. Blend. Add vanilla seeds or a drop of brandy, if you fancy.

HERE'S HOW IT WORKS:

Finely chop some ripe fruit. Pop it into a plastic tub. Freeze.

Break up or chop the frozen pieces, if they're stuck together. Tip into a food-processor or blender.

Blitz until all the fruit is chopped up and the mixture starts to come together into an icy, smooth, creamy paste.

You'll have to process it for a good bit — as you do the fruit will start to melt a little bit, which helps the fruit come together and gives it a softer, creamier texture. Serve immediately. (Sadly, they don't refreeze but they're so quick to whip up that it's easy to make them fresh.)

HAPPY ENDINGS

On the whole, puddings are viewed as treats. They're not something we need but they're a pleasurable tickle for the tastebuds. Because of this, we tend to dismiss any nutritional value a pudding may offer. But in Graham Harvey's book, *We Want Real Food*, he notes that in nature, sweetness is often linked to rich sources of essential trace elements, such as zinc, magnesium, copper and boron, as well as sugar. He says that our hunter-gatherer ancestors had an evolutionary advantage in developing a sweet-tooth. It was a means of selecting the ripest fruits which were at their most nutritious. If you choose the right ingredients, puddings can be good for you, and still taste indulgent.

Throughout writing this book I've craved coffee and cake. At the beginning, I was sitting down writing about why we should eat less meat while munching chocolate brownies washed down by café lattes. Coffee chains have exploited our cravings for caffeine and sugar in their beverages and as David A Kessler points out in *The End Of Overeating: Taking Control Of Our Insatiable Appetite*, 'The warm milk harks back to the primal instinct of

You can cut 90kg of CO2 a year by drinking your tea or coffee black. To illustrate: a cup of black tea or coffee has a carbon footprint of 21g CO2 emissions, whereas the production of a large cafè latte has a carbon footprint of 340g CO2.

infants. Yet, what they offer doesn't satisfy what our bodies are really crying out for: wholesome nutrition.'

There's another problem here, too. It soon became obvious to me the milk in lattes and the butter and eggs in brownies have the same sustainability and health implications that meat does.

The average latte, for instance, contains 250ml of milk. Having three of these a day (roughly what I used to consume) is the carbon equivalent of flying half way across Europe. Drinking so much milk is not healthy, for us or for the cows. Weaning myself off café delicacies has probably been the biggest change I've made to my diet while writing this book. But I haven't given up cake or coffee. I just have them less often and when I do I fully appreciate and savour them.

Ripe, seasonal fruit has filled the gap. It's sweet, and loaded with goodness. Growing fruit is environmentally beneficial too, as wildlife can also feast on it. It is early autumn as I write this and sharing blackberries from the hedgerow with a robin is far more fulfilling than eating a biscuit from a cellophane pack. As a bonus, the blackberries are free.

I used to spend a lot of money in cafés but I've reinvested much of this in buying a weekly seasonal fruit box, which gets delivered to my door each Monday. Instead of sitting in a café, I take more time to go for walks and forage for fruits. Rediscovering fruit has inspired the recipes in this chapter. There is sugar in the recipes but I've trimmed the amount used, relying more on the fruits to shine through with their own natural sweetness.

By no means are all these puddings completely virtuous. Like all the recipes in this book, they're a healthy balance of naughty and nice.

The chocolate manufacturer Cadbury has quantified the greenhouse gas emitted during the course of producing one 50g bar of milk chocolate. The production of the milk (which makes up 25 per cent by weight of the bar's contents) contributes 60 per cent to its overall GHG emissions.

Summer pudding with hot vanilla honey

I once had a slice of a summer pudding I'd made for breakfast. I guiltily
confessed this to a friend and then thought that this pudding is probably
healthier than jam on toast, as there's so much fruit and relatively little sugar.
It's also a beautiful way of celebrating summer berries.

Traditionally, it's served with a puddle of cream, but here I've paired the cold
pudding with a trickle of warmed vanilla-infused honey. The contrast of hot
and cold is delightful and it makes the pudding dairy-free.

SERVES 6

1kg mixture of berries and
currants

100g caster sugar

½ vanilla pod, seeds scraped
(save the pod for the honey)

8 thin slices of bread cut from
a good white loaf, crusts
removed

100ml honey

a few sprigs of fresh mint

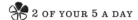 2 OF YOUR 5 A DAY

Quarter or halve the berries, depending on size, and put in a saucepan.
Add the sugar and vanilla. Heat gently.

Cook for 4–5 minutes, stirring frequently until the sugar is dissolved,
the fruits are soft but still retain some of their shape, and there are
plenty of juices in the pan.

Use about six slices of bread to line the base and sides of a 1.2-litre
pudding basin or decent-sized plastic bowl with a flat bottom and tall,
rounded sides (one that looks big enough to hold all the fruit).

Cut and trim the slices so the basin is lined in a fairly even layer with
no gaps.

Use a slotted spoon to nestle the fruit into the basin. Drizzle a bit of juice
over and refrigerate the rest. Cover the fruit with the last two slices of
bread, trimming them to fit. Coap with a saucer that fits just inside the
rim of the basin and weigh down with a jam jar. Refrigerate overnight.

Turn the pudding out onto a serving plate, and brush it all over with the
reserved juice until the pudding is fully saturated. Put aside. Warm the
honey in a pan with the vanilla pod. If the mixture gets too thick, add a
drop of water.

Serve with extra berries if you like. Drizzle the hot honey over the top.
Finish with fresh mint, or serve with a refreshing mint tea.

Almond apple crumble

As soon as the first chill of autumn blows in, I start rustling up crumbles using the apples that appear on my doorstep. Like a summer pudding, this one too is packed full of healthy, seasonal fruit. Feel free to add even more fruit, tumbling in a few plums or pears. It's a great way to use up any bruised or fading fruits.

SERVES 4–6

100g plain white flour for topping, plus 1 tablespoon for filling

100g rolled oats

a pinch of sea salt

75g caster sugar, plus 1 tablespoon for filling

75ml almond oil

6 tablespoons flaked almonds

a pinch of cinnamon, ginger, scraping of vanilla seeds or crushed cardamom seeds

6 apples, peeled, cored and cut into chunky pieces

a splash of brandy (optional)

 1.5 OF YOUR 5 A DAY

Preheat the oven to 180°C/gas mark 4.

Make the topping by mixing the flour, oats, sugar and a pinch of salt. Drizzle over the almond oil and rub in until it resembles wet sand. Add the almonds and a pinch of cinnamon or any other sweet spice you're in the mood for.

Place the fruit, sugar, brandy (if using) and a dash more of your preferred spice straight into the baking dish. Fold everything together. Dust flour over and gently combine the mixture. Pile the topping on.

Place in the oven for 30–45 minutes, or until the top is nicely golden. Serve warm with a glass of dessert wine. Bliss.

Mexican chocolate mousse

Forget eggs and cream – you can turn a ripe avocado into chocolate mousse. Honest. Nothing will make you feel more smug than eating avocado for dessert.

SERVES 4

2 ripe avocados

4 tablespoons unsweetened cocoa powder or raw cacao

4 tablespoons honey or maple syrup

2–3 tablespoons almond milk

a pinch cinnamon

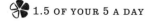 1.5 OF YOUR 5 A DAY

Scoop the avocado flesh into a blender. Add the cocoa, honey, water, and cinnamon. Blitz until smooth. Taste and add more cocoa, honey and/or water if needed. Chill and serve with ripe pears or berries.

Dark raspberry truffles

I've used coconut milk instead of cream in these silky truffles but you really can't taste the difference. I blind-tested these on friends to see if they could note the difference and their only comment was: 'Wow, the raspberries are really lovely in these!'

MAKES 12 TRUFFLES

80g (about 5 tablespoons) fresh raspberries

200g dark chocolate, roughly chopped

100ml coconut milk

cocoa powder, icing sugar or chopped nuts

✿ 1 OF YOUR 5 A DAY WHEN SERVED WITH A HANDFUL OF FRUIT

Crush the raspberries until they're a puréed mush. Do this with a fork or the back of a spoon.

Place a frying pan over medium heat. Place a metal or glass bowl on top of the pan (this will gently warm the bowl – it's a simpler take on the bain-marie).

Add the chocolate and coconut milk to the bowl. Gently stir the contents as it warms until all the chocolate has just melted. Take off the heat. Fold the raspberries through.

Chill the mixture in the fridge until it is firm for about 1 hour. (If you're in a rush, pop the mixture in the freezer. It should firm in 30 minutes.) Scoop into little balls using a teaspoon. Gently and quickly, roll them between your hands — if you handle them too long they'll start to melt. Roll in chopped almonds or dust with cocoa powder. Refrigerate the rolled truffles until ready to serve.

Serve with mixed berries or a selection of seasonal fruit.

Rice pudding with seasonal fruit

A creamy rice pudding is a great carrier for fruit. This one is made with coconut milk instead of milk or cream. It works well as you don't run the risk of having that unfavourable tang of overheated milk. The coconut flavour does come through and works beautifully with the vanilla and seasonal fruit.

SERVES 4

400ml tin coconut milk

400ml cold water

½ vanilla pod, seeds scraped

3 tablespoons golden caster sugar

150g risotto or pudding rice

1 OF YOUR 5 A DAY

Place the coconut milk with the water in a pan, then stir in the vanilla seeds, vanilla pods and the caster sugar.

Heat gently until the sugar dissolves. Bring to the boil. Reduce the heat to a gentle simmer.

Place the rice in another pan and heat for 1–2 minutes. Stir in a third of the warm coconut milk and bring to a simmer, stirring constantly until nearly all the milk has been absorbed. Gradually ladle in the rest of the milk, again stirring continually and ensuring each addition has been fully absorbed. Keep going until the rice is tender, about 20 minutes.

Now for the fruit. Below are a few seasonal ideas

WINTER **HONEYED CARDAMOM ORANGES**

This is delicious. Segment 4 oranges, making sure you collect all the juices as well. Mix with crushed seeds from 3 cardamom pods. Drizzle a little bit of honey over. Ladle the rice into bowls and spoon the honeyed oranges over the top.

SUMMER **FRESH STRAWBERRIES**

While your rice pudding simmers away, trim the tops off and quarter 350g strawberries. Mix with a pinch of golden caster sugar. You can either fold the strawberries through the rice while it's still in the pan, or spoon the rice into bowls and top with the strawberries. A dusting of toasted flaked almonds makes a lovely finishing touch.

SPRING **RHUBARB COMPOTE**

Cut 350g rhubarb into 2–3cm hunks and place in a saucepan. Dust 2 tablespoons golden caster sugar over the top. Pour in enough water to just cover the rhubarb. Simmer for 10 minutes, or until the rhubarb is tender. Ladle the rice into bowls and spoon over the top. Use any excess rhubarb juices as a cordial (i. e. store in a jar in the fridge and dilute with water for a refreshing drink).

AUTUMN **FRESH FIGS**

Plump autumn figs don't really need embellishments. To give them a warmer, earthier backdrop, swap the vanilla in the rice for a few star anise, a cinnamon stick and three crushed cardamom pods. Continue with the rice recipe. When it's done, ladle into bowls and top each bowl with slices from a fresh, plump fig. Finish with toasted walnuts and a little drizzle of honey.

Café

I love cake and café lattes, but such treats are heavy with butter, eggs and of course, milk. All these things count when it comes to eating less meat. But who wants to give up cake? Here are a couple of lovely butter- and egg-free recipes that will satisfy your sweet tooth while also delivering half a portion of fruit and veg.

Coco Cocoa

I must admit defeat when trying to find a wonderful alternative to cow's milk in a café latte. Nothing compares. So I still have proper milky lattes, but now I have them twice a week, rather than 2–3 times a day.

SERVES 1

75ml coconut milk

1 tablespoon cocoa powder

1 teaspoon honey

75ml water

1 tablespoon rum (optional)

1 OR YOUR 5 A DAY IF SERVED WITH A HANDFUL OF STRAWBERRIES OR A PEAR

Warm the coconut milk. Whisk in the cocoa and honey and simmer until dissolved. Top up with water and rum, if using. Warm through. Serve with a handful of fresh strawberries (3–4) or a ripe pear.

VARIATIONS

COCO LATTE No need to measure. Simply make a strong pot or cafetière of coffee. Fill your mug two-thirds full and top with coconut milk. Lovely alongside a handful of dates or a ripe pear.

COCO MOCHA Melt a square of chocolate into a Coco Latte and add a crushed cardamom pod or a touch of vanilla, or swirl with a cinnamon stick to add a little layer of spice. Delicious served with dried mango.

Chocolate banana bread

Banana bread is one of my favourite afternoon treats. This version is made with coconut milk instead of eggs and butter. It offers just a hint of coconut so is by no means overpowering. The chocolate and bananas are the real stars here, and the latter gives you a decent half portion of fruit.

MAKES 1 LOAF, ENOUGH FOR 8 GENEROUS SLICES

olive oil

a spoonful of flour to coat your loaf tin

3 very ripe bananas, well mashed

75g golden caster sugar

75g honey

225g coconut milk

250g plain white, flour

½ teaspoon bicarbonate of soda

½ teaspoon salt

½ teaspoon cinnamon

4 cardamom pods, seeds finely ground (optional)

½ teaspoon fresh grated ginger (optional)

100g bar dark chocolate, chopped into 1cm hunks

50g chopped nuts (optional)

✿ GIVES YOU A 0.5 NUDGE TOWARDS YOUR 5 A DAY

Preheat the oven to 180°C/gas mark 4. Brush the inside of a loaf tin with oil and dust with flour. Turn and tap the tin to coat the bottom and all the sides.

Mush the bananas in a large bowl. Add the sugar, honey and coconut milk, and stir until well mixed.

Sift in the flour, bicarbonate of soda, salt and spices and stir to combine. Add the chocolate and fold it through until evenly dispersed. Stir in the nuts, if using.

Tip the mixture into the prepared tin and bake for 50 minutes to 1 hour, or until a skewer inserted in the middle comes out free of batter (you'll probably have a bit of melted chocolate on it!).

Let the banana bread cool for at least 10 minutes before tipping it out of the tin.

VARIATION

BANANA BLUEBERRY MUFFINS Follow the instructions above. Use one banana instead of three. Omit the chocolate and spices. Add 200g whole, fresh blueberries and the seeds from ½ a vanilla pod or 1 teaspoon vanilla extract instead. Pour into a lined muffin tin that serves 12. Bake for 25–30 minutes, or until a skewer comes out clean.

Honeyed carrot cupcakes

My son loves to help me bake and when I made these he remarked, 'Mummy, there are no eggs or butter in these cakes!' At three, he's already been conditioned to think that these are baking essentials. Well into my 30s, I've only just discovered that they're not.

My new ingredient, as you'll see in many of the sweet recipes in this book, is coconut milk. It does the job of binding the mixture and giving it moisture.

MAKES 6 (THE RECIPE EASILY DOUBLES TO MAKE A DOZEN CUPCAKES)

100ml honey

150ml coconut milk

125g plain white, stoneground flour

½ teaspoon bicarbonate of soda

¼ teaspoon baking powder

¼ teaspoon salt

½ teaspoon ground cinnamon

¼ teaspoon ground ginger

1 medium carrot, finely grated

2 tablespoons chopped walnuts

2 tablespoons raisins

❀ 1 CUPCAKE GIVES YOU 0.5 OF YOUR 5 A DAY

Preheat the oven to 180°C/gas mark 4. Line a muffin tin with 6 cupcake liners.

Whisk together the honey and coconut milk. Sift in the flour, bicarbonate of soda, baking powder, salt and spices. Mix until smooth. Fold in the carrots, walnuts and raisins.

Divide the mix between the cupcake liners. Bake for 25–30 minutes, until a knife inserted through the centre of one comes out clean.

INDEX

✿Acknowledgements

Juggling a book project with work and family is no mean feat, so first and foremost, I'd like to thank my lovely husband Robbie and son Rory for setting off on weekend adventures so I could research, cook and write this book. Another thank you goes to my family and my Gipsy Hill friends for helping me test and develop the recipes – and a special thanks to my dear friend Tina and her husband Ian Archer for their feedback and Maya Gold Chilli recipe.

I'm extremely grateful to Keith Abel and all my lovely colleagues at Abel & Cole for being so supportive and inspiring.

My editor Jenny Wheatley deserves a special mention for being so incredibly patient, allowing me to develop the book at the pace of a snail. The designer, Lawrence Morton, must also be mentioned for his grace in shaping my rambling text in an elegant layout, and to Tim Hopgood for his brilliant illustrations.

Thank you to Linda Tubby, Peter Cassidy and Roisin Nield for making my food look so stunning.

Finally, I owe a lifetime of gratitude to my mother, my granny, sisters and brother for being such amazing cooks. I've learned so much from all of you over the years.

REFERENCES

[p6] 'Meat and Dairy Production and Consumption, Food Climate Research Network', Tara Garnett, Centre for Environmental Strategy, University of Surrey, November 2007

[pp6, 8–9, 16] 'The Global Benefits of Eating Less Meat', Mark Gold, Compassion in World Farming Trust, 2004

[pp6, 10–12] World Health Organisation, www.who.int

[pp6, 16, 164] 'What's Feeding Our Food', Friends of the Earth, December 2009

[pp8, 144] 'Putting Meat Back in Its Place', Mark Bittman, *New York Times,* 11 June 2008

[pp8–9] 'Food, Livestock Production, Energy, Climate Change, and Health', *The Lancet*, Colin D. Butler, Anthony J. McMichael, John W. Powles, Ricardo Uauy, 13 September 2007

[pp8, 16] *Diet for a Small Planet*, Frances Moore Lappé, Ballantine Books Inc, 1976

[pp9, 207] 'Cooking Up a Storm', Tara Garnett, Food Climate Research Network Centre for Environmental Strategy, University of Surrey, September 2008

[pp9–10, 114] World Cancer Research Fund, www.wcrf-uk.org

[p10] 'Food, Nutrition, Physical Activity, and the Prevention of Cancer', World Cancer Research Fund/American Institute for Cancer Research, Washington DC, 2007

[p10] U.K. Department of Health Annual Report 2007

[p16] 'Eating the Planet, Friends of the Earth and Compassion in World Farming', November 2009

[p16] 'U.S. Could Feed 800 Million People with Grain that Livestock Eat', David Pimental, *Cornell University Science News*, 1997

[pp 16, 164–165] *Righteous Porkchop*, Nicolette Hahn Niman, Collins Living, 2009

[pp16, 30] *Eating Animals*, Jonathan Safran Foer, Little, Brown and Company, 2009

[pp16, 86] PBS Frontline, Modern Meat, www.pbs.org/wgbh/pages/ frontline/shows/meat

[pp16, 46–47, 114–115, 186, 206] *We Want Real Food*, Graham Harvey, Constable, 2006

[pp16, 87] 'Silent Invasion – The Hidden Use of GM Crops in Livestock Feed', Soil Association, 2007

[p16] 'Identifying the Real Winners from U.S. Agricultural Policies, Global Development and Environment Institute', Timothy A. Wise, Tufts University, December 2005

[p17] 'How Cows [Grass-Fed Only] Could Save the Planet', Lisa Abend, *Time*, 25 January 2010

[pp17, 164–165] Eat Wild, www.eatwild.com

[p17] *Pasture Perfect*, Jo Robinson, Vashon Island Press, 18 July 2007

[p17] 'A Review of Fatty Acid Profiles and antioxidant content in grass-fed and grain-fed beef', *Journal Animal Science*, March 2010

[pp17, 46] *Meat: A Benign Extravagance*, Simon Fairlie, Permanent Publications, 2010

[p33] *A Cowboy in the Kitchen*, Grady Spears and Rob Walsh, Ten Speed Press, 1998

[p46] 'Guardian of the Hills', Rachael Oakden, *Country Living*, May 2010

[pp46–47, 130–131] *The River Cottage Meat Book*, Hugh Fearnley-Whittingstall, Hodder & Stoughton, 2004

[p66] American Livestock Breeds Conservancy, www.albc-usa.org

[p66] Rare Breeds Survival Trust, www.rbst.org.uk

[pp66–67] *Fat*, Jennifer McLagan, Ten Speed Press/Jacqui Small, 2008

[p67] 'Heritage pork', Dara Moskowitz, *USA Today*, 26 January 2007

[pp67, 115] Laverstoke Park Farm, www.laverstokepark.co.uk

[p86] The British Poultry Council, www.poultry.uk.com

[p86] 'The chicken, the factory farm and the supermarket: the emergence of the modern poultry industry in Britain', Andrew C Godley and Bridget Williams, University of Reading, 2007

[p86] 'An HSUS Report: Human Health Implications of Intensive Poultry Production and Avian Influenza', The Humane Society of the United States, 2008

[p87] 'Eating Up the Amazon', Greenpeace, April 2006

[p87] Pastured Poultry Products: Summary, Sustainable Agriculture Research and Education [SARE], 1999

[p94] *Waste*, Tristram Stuart, Penguin, 2009

[p103] *The Atlas of Food,* Erik Millstone and Tim Lang, The Earthscan Atlas Series, 2008,

[p114] 'The Significance of the Issuance of the 5th Revision of the Japanese Standard Tables of Food Components on Study and Research on Vitamins and Diseases', O. Igarashi, 36th Vitamin Information Center Press Seminar, Tokyo, 2001

[p115] 'A Farm for the Future', directed by Tim Green and Rebecca Hosking, 2008–2009

[p130] *The Pantropheon*, Alexis Soyer, Reprint of 1853 ed. published by Simpkin, Marshall, Paddington Press Ltd, 1977

[p130] *An Edible History of Humanity*, Tom Standage, Atlantic Books; 2009

[pp130–131, 165] *Forgotten Skills of Cooking*, Darina Allen, Kyle Cathie, 2009

[pp140–141] 'Fish Farming's Growing Dangers', Ken Stier, *Time*, 19 September 2007

[pp 140–141] 'End of the Line', directed by Rupert Murray, 2009

[pp140–141, 151, 155] *The River Cottage Fish Book*, Hugh Fearnley-Whittingstall and Nick Fisher, Bloomsbury, 2007

[pp140–141] Fish Online, www.fishonline.org

[pp148, 152] Seafood and Eat It, www. seafoodandeatit.co.uk

[p164] 'Effect of Free-Range Feeding on Omega-3 Fatty Acids and Alpha-Tocopherol Content and Oxidative Stability of Eggs', C. J. Lopez- Bote, R. Sanz Arias, A.I. Rey, A. Castano, B. Isabel, J. Thos, *Animal Feed Science and Technology*, 72, pp33–40, 1998

[p164] 'Pastured Egg Nutrient Tests', Tabitha Alterman, *Mother Earth News*, February/March 2009

[p164] 'Studies on the Composition of Food, the Chemical Composition of Eggs Produced Under Battery, Deep Litter and Free-Range Conditions', A. Tolan et al, *British Journal of Nutrition*, 31:185, 1974

[p165] British Hen Welfare Trust, www.bhwt.org.uk

[pp165, 186] Compassion in World Farming, www.ciwf.org.uk

[p186] 'The Revolution Will Not Be Pasteurized', Nathanael Johnson, *Harper's*, April 2008

[p186] 'Quantitative Secretion and Maximal Secretion Capacity of Retinol, Betacarotene and Alpha-Tocopherol into Cows' Milk', S.K. Jensen, *Journal of Dairy Research*, 66: 4, pp511–522, 1999

[p186] 'Recording and Evaluation of Fertility Traits in UK Dairy Cattle', MDC-funded research project awarded to SAC, the University of Reading and the Roslin Institute, 2001

[p186] 'Countryside in Crisis: How Dairy Farmers are Milked Dry', Olga Craig, *Daily Telegraph*, 6 June 2010

[p186] 'Mud, Sweat and Tractors', BBC4, 2009

[pp186–187] 'Britain's First Milk Factory', Alex Renton, Word of Mouth Blog, *Guardian*, 2 March 2010

[p187] 'The Food We Waste', Waste & Resources Action Programme, April 2008

Spoonfed Suppers, www.spoonfedsuppers.com [p201]

[pp206–207] *End of Overeating*, David Kessler, Penguin, 2010

[pp206–207] *How Bad Are Bananas?*, Mike Berners-Lee, Profile, 2010